3

WITHDRAWN

SCHOOL OF ORIENTAL AND AFRICAN STUDIES

UNIVERSITY OF LONDON

Jordan Lectures in Comparative Religion

VIII

The Louis H. Jordan Bequest

The will of the Rev. Louis H. Jordan provided that the greater part of his estate should be paid over to the School of Oriental and African Studies to be employed for the furtherance of Studies in Comparative Religion, to which his life had been devoted. Part of the funds which thus became available was to be used for the endowment of a Louis H. Jordan Lectureship in Comparative Religion. The lecturer is required to deliver a course of six or eight lectures for subsequent publication. The first series of lectures was delivered in 1951.

JORDAN LECTURES 1967

The Privilege of Man

*A Theme in Judaism,
Islam and Christianity*

by

KENNETH CRAGG

UNIVERSITY OF LONDON
THE ATHLONE PRESS
1968

Published by
THE ATHLONE PRESS
UNIVERSITY OF LONDON
at 2 Gower Street, London W C I
Distributed by Constable & Co Ltd
12 *Orange Street, London* W C 2

U.S.A.
Oxford University Press Inc
New York

Canada
Oxford University Press
Toronto

485 17408 1

Printed in Great Britain by
WILLIAM CLOWES AND SONS, LIMITED
LONDON AND BECCLES

For
J O H N
and
G A Z A
his
birthplace

PREFACE

The invitation to prepare the Jordan Lectures, 1967, reached me during a sabbatical leave at Union Theological Seminary in New York, and their delivery coincided with my final term as Warden of St Augustine's College, Canterbury. The task was one I anticipated with both trepidation and eagerness. There was the formidable sequence, in the Lectureship, of substantial themes and expert scholarship, which I was ill-equipped to maintain. But there was also the sense that a School, justly reputed for its many contributions to oriental and African studies in all the manifold areas that academic orientalia and Africana now entail, had in this Lectureship an obligation to living religion—a sphere all too readily avoided by academics. I did not, therefore, wish to propose something merely erudite or theoretical. I felt an impulse to come to grips, if possible, with contemporary human experience and set the comparisons, enjoined upon the Jordan Lecturer, in that field. It seemed to me that fruitful Jewish-Christian-Islamic study might best be found in the theme of man.

I had for long been intrigued by the Biblical concept of human 'dominion' and the kindred Quranic doctrine of Adam as the 'caliph'. I toyed with the title: 'In Stead of God', deliberately phrased and spelled that way. This would have fitted but would plainly have risked misleading the reader. 'The Caliphate' would not have suggested, at least in advance of the elucidation of its subtlety, anything more than the political and the historical which, with apologies, is not its primary meaning. 'Considering man' seemed at once too jejune and pretentious. 'In Lieu of God', though strictly accurate, would have been archaic and so, again, deceptive. Finally I came upon the thought of 'The Privilege of Man' and it seemed satisfactory, though it was only on my way to the first lecture that a billboard told me the word had become the title of an intriguing, popular film, about the manipulative role of a pop-singer idol, in a gullible society of mass emotion.

The term is not perfect, but it suffices. The first lecture aimed to set in focus the present time, and the second to introduce caliphal man in power under God, and the third to explore the common Semitic prototype in Abraham. The next three lectures, being the main body of 'comparison', ponder the Jewish, Muslim and Christian accents on man, in election, in the prophet-state, and in grace and sonship. The two concluding lectures return to the contemporary meaning of the crisis of man, and to the relevance of faiths which forbid his absolute pretensions yet call him to the servant-mastery.

Some few weeks after the Lectures were given, I chanced to participate in the biennial Anglo-Scandinavian Theological Conference at Cambridge and listened there to a paper in which there occurred this sentence: 'Every branch of science contributes in its own way to the displacement of man from a position of privilege.' The writer went on to cite astronomical or geological time and to tell how 'biochemistry revealed that there was no privilege left in life', and relativity disqualified even geometric measures. I am unrepentant. It is true, of course, that we must allow a sort of Kantian ego-centricity to all our knowing and agree that the general statements we make about the nature and purpose of the universe have their shape from our human knowing, and that we must reserve some extra-personal dimension of things as they might be if we, who know them and 'live' them, were other than humans are. Yet this very *caveat* of honesty is a sort of triumph. We are enough aware of such world other than ours to pay it the tribute of our reservations. In that sense we are already true to it. And whether so or not, inescapably the life we lead, the world in which we move, give us back the privilege, even though it be also the paradox that we know and know not, that we reign and do not reign. It is exactly such reservation from the ultimate pride that the word 'privilege' intends. We need the sovereignty of God if there is to be a proper honesty, not to say benediction, in our own.

It remains for me to thank the Director and Professors of the School of Oriental and African Studies, for their courtesy, forbearance and generous hospitality—the Director who presided at the Jordan dinner and Professors J. B. Segal (Head of the Department of the Near and Middle East), C. F. Beckingham (Professor of Islamic Studies) and D. J. Wiseman (Professor of Assyriology) who took the chair at the sessions. To the Secretary and the participants I am grateful for many kindnesses. May I be allowed to add my appreciation of the opportunity, over many years, of reading in the S.O.A.S. Library, to which I owe much?

How right that a book on this theme should be inscribed, with warm affection, to our first-born son, who taught me so much about it, when he came to us in the glad mystery of family, while we were 'refugees' in Gaza. The sorrows of that strip of territory in two decades deserve to be the symbol of the other, and the tragic, reckoning with which men have to do, in the trust of man. I can only hope that, despite their inadequacies, these Jordan Lectures may have in some measure achieved the intention of Louis H. Jordan, their founder, for the living business of faith and the faiths. There is no sterner test of it than in the toils and tribulations of that part of the world with which the name of his Lectureship might so readily be confused.

Canterbury, July 1967   K. C.

CONTENTS

ACKNOWLEDGEMENTS

Permission to quote from the works named is hereby acknowledged to the following:

Bowes & Bowes (Publishers) Ltd.: *The Disinherited Mind* by Erich Heller.

Cambridge University Press: *Science and the Modern World* by A. N. Whitehead; *Political Thought in Medieval Islam* by E. I. J. Rosenthal and *Philosophy and Myth in Karl Marx* by Robert Tucker.

Jonathan Cape Ltd.: *A Farewell to Arms* and *To Have and to Have Not* with acknowledgement to the Executors of the Ernest Hemingway Estate.

Chatto & Windus Ltd.: *The Elizabethan World Picture* by E. M. W. Tillyard; *A Fable* by William Faulkner and *Collected Poems of Wilfred Owen* (by courtesy of Mr Harold Owen).

T. & T. Clark Ltd.: *Church Dogmatics* by Karl Barth.

William Collins, Sons & Co. Ltd.: The Gelineau version of *The Psalms*.

Cornell University Press: *Ideas of Arab Nationalism* by H. Z. Nuseibeh.

Djambatan Ltd.: *Urubah and Religion* by I. R. al Faruqi.

Faber & Faber Ltd.: *Markings* by Dag Hammarskjold and *The Rebel* by Albert Camus.

Calder & Boyars, Ltd.: *Malone Dies* by Samuel Beckett.

East & West Library: *Moses* by Martin Buber.

Hamish Hamilton Ltd.: *Iron in the Soul* by Jean-Paul Sartre.

William Heinemann Ltd.: *The Grapes of Wrath* by John Steinbeck and *Women in Love* by D. H. Lawrence.

Hutchinson & Co. Ltd.: *The Modern Novel* by Paul West.

Macdonald and Co. (Publishers) Ltd.: *A Glastonbury Romance* by John Cowper Powys.

Methuen and Co. Ltd.: *The Art of the Soluble* by P. B. Medawar; *High Dam at Aswan* by Tom Little and *Wind, Sand and Stars* by Saint-Éxupèry.

Holt, Rinehart & Winston Inc. and Laurence Pollinger Ltd.: Three poems from *Collected Poems of Robert Frost* (published by Jonathan Cape Ltd.).

I

Contemporary Man:
'I Lack Nothing Except Myself'

'THINK of what you can do with what there is', wrote Ernest Hemingway in *The Old Man and the Sea*.[1] An almost conversational suggestion, it serves well enough for our present purpose, though its own setting may be grim. The concern of all that follows is to explore the meaning of man exercising power with his context, to borrow for this end the central Biblical and Quranic theme of human 'dominion' and relate it to prevailing contemporary experience both of technological authority and human disquiet. 'What there is' and 'what you can do' cover between them the whole vast triumphant and desolating business of mankind in the world.

It would, of course, be possible to choose other beginnings. This, for example, being the opening paragraph of John Cowper Powys' longest novel: *A Glastonbury Romance*:

At the striking of noon on a certain fifth of March, there occurred within a causal radius of Brandon railway station, and yet beyond the deepest pools of emptiness between the uttermost stellar systems, one of those infinitesimal ripples in the creative silence of the First Cause which will always occur when an exceptional stir of heightened consciousness agitates any living organism in this astronomical universe.[2]

That, at least, is one way of taking a narrative plunge into a ripening of acquaintance and affection between a John and a Mary in a Somersetshire town. Or one can initiate a story in the manner of Samuel Beckett:

I shall soon be quite dead in spite of it all. Perhaps next month. Then it will be the month of April or of May. For the year is still young, a thousand little signs tell me so. Perhaps I am wrong . . . I would not put it past me to pant on to the Transfiguration . . . but I do not think

---

[1] New York, 1952, p. 122.   [2] London, 1933, p. 1.

so, I do not think I am wrong in saying that these rejoicings will take place in my absence this year.[1]

Or again, and unsurpassed in all literature as an opening, there is Herman Melville's inspired: 'Call me Ishmael . . .' in *Moby Dick*, with the tense unfolding drama of the Pequod and one man's relentless pursuit of the great whale, told through the record of the single, surviving witness, that same Ishmael, saved by a floating coffin in which

. . . for almost one whole day and night, I floated on a soft and dirge like main . . . On the second day, a sail drew near, nearer, and picked me up at last. It was the devious cruising Rachel that, in her retracing search after her own missing children, only found another orphan.[2]

Between the beginning and that end every reader puzzles his way towards the meaning of the mystery of man as Melville intended darkly to propose it in the passion of his Captain Ahab. How, in the author's own word, do we 'subtilize' our minds, to take in the disclosure of mankind in the vicissitudes of a protracted voyage and the tragedy of a magnificent perversity?

Our business here, of course, is not to start a novel, but simply to move from ruminations about how novelists have done so, into our own academic theme. Yet the leaves, opening leaves, from these books serve by these occasions to kindle the imagination to countless other situations of men and of environment in inter-relation. Mariners and the sea; railways, lovers and the stars; the prospect of death in the rebirth of spring; religious symbols whether as clues for the wistful or names for the casual; twelve o'clock striking in the silence of infinity—each is a token fragment of the literature of life. Shakespeare, maybe, has it best of all when he draws back the curtain on *Hamlet* with the cry of an agitated sentry at the changing of the castle guard: 'Who's there?' and the play's own answer: 'man, that piece of work'.

It is this theme of the identity and the context of man that is intended in these Chapters. The hope is to study the human

---

[1] From *Malone Dies*, in Three Novels, New York, 1965 edition, p. 179.

[2] The opening and closing sentences of *Moby Dick*.

tenancy of the world, in the light of the underlying Biblical and Quranic concept of man as the proper imperialist, the true dominion-holder in the earth. The three religions concerned here, in contrasted yet also deeply unifying terms, see man as the vicegerent[1] set over things under God, so that the stuff of his empire is also the sacrament or substance of his worship. The Jordan Lectures, strictly speaking, enjoin a bilateral study or theme-comparison between two religions only. But it is a valid claim that the triangular relationship in which we are here involved is well seen as a single, unitary study. It would violate its whole nature to restrict it arbitrarily to Judaism and Christianity, or Christianity and Islam. Indeed, in wider fields, one of the fascinating aspects of our current 'ecumenical' theology is the way in which the 'Christian' reach of relation, demanding at crucial points to take in Judaism also, finds it can hardly stay there, and exclude Islam. We have, however, no hesitation in availing ourselves of our founder's prescript and not incorporate here the faiths of further Asia and of Africa—for all their experience of the dimensions of man.

The phrase 'the privilege of man' is meant to describe this human status as the three monotheisms have broadly received and seen it. The distinctiveness of the 'different law', the enjoyment of right and advantage, the possession of immunities, having the pattern of things in one's favour, and the quality of trust-bestowal and honour-boundness—all these are caught and hinted in the Latin *privilegium*. Not all the shades of its English derivative are apposite, but the general sense, it may be hoped, will emerge clearly enough in the sequel. Our task is to ponder and examine the Biblical and Quranic prerogative of man, the double trust whereby competence and obligation move together in the meaning of existence. Our duty is to this theme in a proper isolation from all the complex questions of psychology and anthropology which proliferate around the human topic. There is here a single

---

[1] It is odd that the two derivatives 'vicegerent' and 'viceregent' should be so close in form as to be taken by some as almost equivalents. The former is preferred here as meaning a delegated authority, not an exercise of 'absent' power.

subject, with sources in scripture and doctrine, and with bearing on the present scene, but reasonably exempt from many separable, if adjacent, themes, about spirit and body, law and sin, and the rest. The concept of human vicegerency suffices as a criterion of expository inclusion. It has to be noted in the documentary terms and then considered in the characteristic forms that Judaism, Islam and Christianity, in that order, have given it. The figure of Abraham, as a great prototype in common, stands eloquently as a preface, one might even say, as a rehearsal, of its nature. We move, in conclusion, towards some attempted resolution of the tensions that belong with the threefold picture of man in the proper behalf of God.

But the immediate need is to catch the present intensity which belongs with the academic theme. The comparison of religions in this field is no mere discourse about the minutiae of terms and doctrines. There is nothing abstract about it. It has nothing to do with archaeology. Rather it bears urgently upon developments in the world around the shrines and on the steadily secularizing trends manifest in the pressures of our day. There is a strenuous prospect confronting the religious temper in the modern world. Theology is on the stretch—if not all theologians are—as rarely before in the history of any of the faiths that are here in view.

By the same tokens, it is probably on man, rather than God, that they can most usefully focus their comparisons and mutual ventures, not because the reality of God is not their ultimate integrity, but because the theme of man is the surest evocation of theological sincerities and searchings in our present circumstances. For this reason we must seek a living, and not simply an academic, authenticity in all that follows. This duty, in turn, demands some reflection on the contemporary human situation—whatever the risk of truism and generalization—in its paradoxical aspect of achievement and dismay. 'I lack nothing', wrote Franz Kafka, 'except myself'.

CONTEMPORARY MAN: POSSESSING THE WORLD

What we do with what there is is more and more radically revising our human tenancy of place and time, more drastically revoking the past and revolutionizing the future than ever any previous generation knew. Immense radio telescopes penetrate beyond the Milky Way to the nebulae in Andromeda and yet more distant galaxies of stars, registering light that left its stellar sources before the remotest terrestrial stirrings of pre-history. With what age then today is man contemporary as he 'sees' the stellar immensities of the universe? Or weigh the techniques of a supersonic aircraft, its whole structure, equipment and performance a concerted triumph of research, imagination and cumulative engineering skill. Or, within the immediate territory of one of our three faiths, consider Kuwait as a concentration of technological achievement—a phenomenal experience of sheer marvel, in the wealth of oil exploitation, the tanker jetties, the massive water distillation, the annual revenues averaging some $3000 per citizen from one commodity, the pleasant luxury of trees and shrubs along the boulevards costing $250 apiece a year to water, and the generous provision of social and educational welfare in the community, and all within a quarter century of a primitive economy unchanging since the days of the Prophet himself. To think of what you can do with what there is makes a delectable reflection in Kuwait.[1]

As it does for any Egyptian, President, technician, labourer or peasant, taking stock of the High Dam at Aswan, which presents no less remarkable occasion for awed congratulation. Here is an act of will that changes the whole rhythm of the life of a great river and, with it, the pulse of an entire nation. It means, one might say, a quite new era in Egypt's relations with the Nile, a new definition to what has always been definitive. The temples of Abu Simbel have been given laborious reprieve but only by the same proud technology that rides high on their inundated past.

The great River Nile will never again be the same in Egypt after 1967. Its waters will no longer burst through the sluices of the old dam and fill the Egyptian channel with rich, brown water. The annual flood,

[1] See Fakhri Shehab in *Modernization of the Arab World*, ed. J. H. Thompson and R. D. Reischauer, New York, 1966, pp. 126-40.

the 'miracle' that through the ages has meant life to the people of Egypt and to this day is still watched in wonderment . . . will not be seen again from that year forward and for ever. The tributaries will lose themselves in Lake Nasser and thereafter it will be by man's will, not God's, that water will be fed to the Egyptian fields.[1]

'By man's and not God's' is an almost automatic, yet still dubious, assumption which we will defer to Chapter VIII. Meanwhile the enthusiasm is entirely right. For in this mastery of the Nile it is fair to find the most compelling symbol of the technological authority of contemporary man. 'The flood', as Tom Little goes on to observe, 'has a transcendent place in history', and lies at the root of the elements of human knowledge, having for its prediction and control excited and required the major achievements of human reckoning and the ordering of their civilization. The traditional *Yaum Wafā' al-Nīl*, the feast of the Nilotic fidelity, of August 22, will become pure archaism and the symbol of the virgin of the waters an empty gesture from a bygone age.

With so inclusive an example it is pointless to add more and the case needs no arguing. Our concern, rather, is with some of the popular consequences, whether in the west or the east, in societies longer or more newly conversant with the scientific revolution. The first is an evident 'alienation' of man from the elemental mysteries and hallowings of his existence. When Marx used this term he had in mind the effects of capitalist production on the human relationship and to aspects of this we will return. But there is danger of a fundamental alienation from reality itself in the current depreciation of the meaning of environment and the forfeiture, through science, unnecessary yet wide-spread, of the sense of the poetry of things. There is what might fairly be called an artificializing, a coarsening, of the human spirit in its handling of the material of experience.

This might readily be substantiated, at some risk perhaps of carping, by the endlessly acquisitive repetitions and criteria of

---

[1] Tom Little, *High Dam at Aswan*, London, 1965, p. 231.

contemporary advertising, with their prostitution of genuine emotions and their well calculated exploitation of human gullibility and competition. It is of course easy to retort that life without amenities could be nothing more than savagery and nakedness, raw meat under a tree, brutish and nasty. But *reductio ad absurdum otiosum* is no answer. The point is the vulgarization of living in the means to it, and the temptation that has come to attach to applied science by which men abandon the primeval wonder. Their very machines seem at once both to proclaim and to degrade their human quality.

The man sitting in the iron seat did not look like a man: gloved, goggled, rubber dust mask over nose and mouth, he was part of a monster, a robot in the seat . . . The monster that sent the tractor out, had somehow got into the driver's hands, into his brain and muscle, had goggled him and muzzled him . . . He could not see the land as it was, he could not smell the land as it smelled: his feet could not stamp the clods or feel the warmth and power of the earth. He sat in an iron seat and stepped on iron pedals . . . He did not know, or own, or trust or beseech the land . . . Behind the harrows, the long seeders—twelve curbed iron penes erected in the foundry, orgasms set by gears, raping methodically, raping without passion . . . And when that crop grew, and was harvested, no man had crumbled a hot clod in his fingers and let the earth sift past his finger tips . . . The land bore under iron and under iron gradually died: for it was not loved or hated . . .[1]

John Steinbeck has the situation rightly here, and with a proper passion. Yet the protest, if it is to be truly made, must not seem some Luddite refusal of the march of change. It is, positively, a call to do battle, in the new sophistication, for the old simplicities. For, if we have a discernment not cheapened by vulgarity, they survive. They even intensify. There is no reason to imagine that the capacity for poetry is somehow annulled by the competence of the machine, that there is a wonder in the heavens for shepherds but none for astronauts. If the latter fail to find it, it is not its absence by which the former were deceived: it is rather the pride

[1] *The Grapes of Wrath*, Stockholm edition, 1943, pp. 41–2.

by which the last are blinded. Science, imaginatively known, far from immunizing men from the springs of worship and mystery, only plunges them more deeply into them. It both enlarges the range of human liabilities and diversifies the sense of imagination's calling.

But only if it is so allowed and it is just here that the contemporary menace is so sharp. A society that is steadily denatured by invention and vulgarity, by ugliness and waste, by noise, by atrophy of worship, needs the greater act of will to be its human self, or contrariwise, is more tempted than its predecessors to acquiesce in its own defeat. The alienation, in either form, has to be deliberately surmounted, in a new assertion of the human *in* the technological, an assertion which neither abdicates the empire, nor abandons the imagination.

The pioneer French aviator-poet, Saint-Éxupèry, captured profoundly in his writings this double vocation of man in this time. Early seized with the wonder of the aeroplane, he knew how to yield to its incredible gift of new dimension to human experience, dimensions of power, perspective, speed and hope. Responding with his own compelling blend of heroism and poetry to the new marvel, he knew how to castigate the sluggish life which could not rise to it. Of the phlegmatic denizens of the towns below him in his fragile craft, he wrote:

You rolled yourself up into a ball in your genteel security, in routine, in the stifling conventions of provincial life, raising a modest rampart against the winds and the tides and the stars . . . You are not dwellers on an errant planet and you do not ask yourselves questions to which there is no answer. You are a petty bourgeois of Toulouse. Nobody grasped you by the shoulder while there was still time . . .[1]

Yet, with all the liberation bestowed by the machine, he did not despise or dismiss '. . . that world where a lamp shines at nightfall on the table and flesh calls to mated flesh, a homely world of love and hopes and memories'.[2] Nor did he scorn the simplicities, even

[1] *Wind, Sand and Stars*, trans. L. Galantière, London, 1940, pp. 14-15.

[2] *Vol de Nuit*, in *Oeuvres*, Paris, 1953, p. 120.

the mediocrities, to which his new empire of skymastery was servant. 'What matter', he wrote of the air mail aboard,

though they hold but the scribblings of tradespeople and nondescript lovers. The interests that dictated them may very well not be worth the embrace of man and storm: but I know what they become once they have been entrusted to the crew, taken over, as the phrase is. If some day the crew are hooked by a cliff it will not have been in the interest of tradespeople that they will have died but in obedience to orders which ennoble the sacks of mail once they are on board . . .[1]

And then, one day, crashed in the desert of Libya, he was able to identify in the face of a nameless bedouin, ignorant of all the subtleties of flight and the lore of the machine, the inclusive image of man. Here, in St Éxupèry's winsome idiom, is the truth of the necessary partnership between the human tools and the human temper. But in other hands than such as his the partnership is being steadily destroyed.

It must be entirely clear that we are in no way arguing here for some withdrawal from the time, some repudiation of the present, as the condition of the human fulness. It is a counsel of despair to imply that God can only be well worshipped on farms, or that to be reverent one has to be primitive. It is no true human imagination that is viable only in seclusion from the city. We are not pleading for some Walden-like exemption from the business of the ordinary world. For, except as a salutary discipline, Thoreau's remedy pretends to save man without men, and the task is both impossible and futile. His sauntering eye, his vivid appreciation of the senses, his eager natural bent, are admirable if duly related. But 'out into the woods . . . to take a new and absolute view of things, empty clean of . . . all institutions of men' is deceptive and delusory. Thoreau in *Walden* is not really meeting life, save by radical revision of its shape. Nature cannot be had without human nature: meaning is not soliloquy, as even Thoreau himself suspected. 'It would be sweet to deal with men more, I can imagine: but where dwell they? Not in fields which I traverse.'[2]

[1] *Wind, Sand and Stars, op. cit.*, pp. 25-6.
[2] Henry Thoreau, *Complete Works*, New York, 1906, Vol. xv, pp. 205 and 362.

The Lawrences and Maughams and Stevensons of literature, who seek out truth in their Mexican or Tahitian sanctuaries, are in false retreat. 'Nature is fine', as Keats wrote, 'but human nature is finer.' The fault, dear Brutus, is not in our cities that we are coarsened things, but in our souls.

The few perhaps may elude the corrosion of humanity in exotic search and find some geographical salvation. But they will not this way save it. Only in a steady, passionate, deliberate acknowledgement of the sacramental dimension, heightened not dissipated by the attainments of science, will they do so. It is this necessity which makes so dubious and damnable the current notion of 'religionless' humanity. For this is to extend a necessary repudiation of superstitious attitudes to an inclusive rejection of the mystery of nature, a proceeding which is either wild enough to dispense with wonder and with poetry, or naïve enough to imagine that somehow the emotions of gladness and wistfulness could live and speak without symbols and without forms. Our deepest battle, whether in the sophisticated west or the bewildered 'older' cultures, is not to scout superstition—which science well enough can do—but rather to build sanctity, and to do so without withdrawal from the world and without exemption from man.

In this task it is useful to be fortified by a sensibly disciplined perspective of the historical. We are too ready for the supposition that current humanity is exceptional and that preceding ages were more simply wrought. We tolerate the easy conclusion that previous times saw 'ages of faith', where doubt was unknown and mystery was all dogmatically labelled. It is sometimes even alleged that the geo-centric universe was a placid abode of human naïveté, all deceived in its own favour by the illusion of self-importance. The notion of unprecedented perplexity dating from our generation needs short shrift from historical honesty.

Far from being dignified and tending to an insolent anthropocentricity, the earth in the Ptolemaic system was the cesspool of the universe . . . Nor did the Ptolemaic system make for any sense of smallness or confinement. It was just as possible in Elizabethan days as later to be terrified by the vast spheres. Caxton's encyclopedist must have taken away the breath of the vulgar quite as effectively as any modern lecturer on the marvels of the heavens: and he uses the same method.[1]

If the sixteenth century is thought to be too near, one may find the same sentiments in Marcus Aurelius, for whom the earth was but a pinpoint in infinite space and like a razor's edge between two eternities. These things were known before Somerset Maugham. In correcting this intoxication with the supposed uniqueness of the present, we do not mean, of course, any stupid refusal of the taxing quality of contemporary complexity. But it is well to avoid easy notions of maturity and adulthood lately dateable, and not to imagine that past ages have monopolies of faith to our exclusion, or we monopolies of despair to theirs. It could even be that they expressed it better and sensed it deeper, 'all in pieces, all cohesion gone'.

> They cannot scare me with their empty spaces
> Between stars—on stars where no human race is.
> I have it in me so much nearer home
> To scare myself with my own desert places.[2]

Robert Frost is admittedly a twentieth-century poet. But the New England out of which his heart spoke is much older and the sentiment is timeless. Only if we admit this essential identity of the human can we rightly measure our own admittedly vexing scene.

We shall do both the more readily if it is also clear that even the times which our comparisons hold simple or submissive had their own share of the will to mastery which we have made so technically sure. What we easily dismiss as 'magic', whether in Europe earlier or Africa later, reveals on closer study a high degree of sophistication. The *will* to mastery which is the crux of technology is very old indeed. The determination to wield environmental control is human, not modern.

Moreover, it is to less progressive ages that we owe the masteries in which we now exult. It is neither frank nor generous

[1] E. M. W. Tillyard, *The Elizabethan World Picture*, London, 1963 edition, pp. 53–4.

[2] Robert Frost, *Complete Poems*, New York, 1949, p. 386.

to assume a lordly superiority where we have only the debt and the advantage of time. Progress, scientifically, is an achievement owed to the less progressive. There is a properly religious honesty, which we badly need, in saying so. The things we readily malign serve to humility better than to pride.

'It needs but a sentence', wrote A. N. Whitehead, and one might perhaps add, a ready mind, '. . . to point out how the habit of definite, exact thought was implanted in the European mind by the long dominance of scholastic logic and scholastic divinity . . . The Middle Ages formed one long training of the intellect of western Europe in the sense of order.'[1]

It is considerations such as these which help to deter a necessary castigation of pre-scientific naïveties from passing over into a brash and summary celebration of modernity. We need not adopt the prevalent illusion that somehow science is not free unless the world is disenchanted, or that the mind cannot be investigative if it is also religious. The 'religious' dissuasions from science, which have been many and deplorable, arising from vested dogmatic interest, from the sort of authority bent only on blind self-conservation, must be truthfully distinguished from the proper postures of worship and awe. The latter are in no sense an incubus on scientific attitudes or enterprise, whatever may have been historically true from time to time about the dogmas in which they found expression. On the contrary, there is in the self-oblation, required of science by the laws of evidence and of conceptual thought, a profoundly religious kinship of spirit with the sense of the sacramental and the awesome. There is no necessary equation between technology and secularity, between competence and profanity. The world is not more readily harnessed for being desacralized. Nor are men truer for being disenchanted.

The truth, rather, is that the more thoroughly and efficiently we exploit and control, the more urgently must we hold in trust. If there is a deep religious potential in the temper of right science, there is an even more insistent necessity of religious awareness in

[1] In *Science and the Modern World*, London, 1948 edition, p. 13. See also Ch. VIII below.

its fruits and their possession. 'What you can do with what there is' in the direct, empirical sense of technological achieving, cries out for what we must do with what there is in the total, doxological, sense—using doxology here for that ultimate referability to joy and worth, of all that is. For our doings are ever more sharply setting, and complicating, the question of our being.

For one thing there are, bewilderingly, so many more of us. Man's increasing management of environment means a steady proliferation of his numbers. It took, perhaps, one million years for the world to reach a billion people, as it did, around the year 1800. In 1967 we are surging forward towards four billion, with the population of the earth doubling every thirty-five years. Every month sees a million more in India alone. These are not simply questions of ecology, of the earth's feasible tolerance of masses. They are also questions of radical meaning. What is man for? Is he to be extinguished by sheer multiplication, denied life by birth itself? And in that ever swelling throng, an ever larger proportion in the cities, so that by the year 2000, only ten per cent will still be villagers and the rest condemned to the alienation, the frustration, the ungovernability, of vast urban colossi. What then of never seeing the arched thrust of the seed, breaking the soft earth into crumbs around it? Robert Frost, who captured that vivid country image, seemed to believe that there was a sign of grace in the fact of number. In 'Our Hold on the Planet' he wrote:

> There is much in nature against us. But we forget:
> Take nature altogether since time began,
> Including human nature, in peace and war,
> And it must be a little more in favor of man,
> Say a fraction of one per cent at the very least,
> Or our number living wouldn't be steadily more,
> Our hold on the planet wouldn't have so increased.[1]

But, even thus modestly, can we still be sure? Is it really a hold on the planet to have so many limpets?

[1] *Op. cit.*, p. 469.

Further, what is becoming of man by dint of dispensability? One of the most bitter ironies in the very prowess of technology is its capacity to make men unnecessary, at least in respect of that by which they have essentially found their meaning, namely work. In the age of computers and cybernation, men have achieved their own redundancy. Machines can more and more become self-regulating, through techniques of analysis, data-selection, computation, error-detection and processing, and all these functions more speedily and accurately than in human hands. Where other revolutions have effectuated immense changes in the human relation to environment, cybernation means disconcerting upheaval in the very relation to the self. What is to be done with the human consequences of an unwanted manpower and with the untried circumstances of inescapable leisure? What will men do with a perpetual sabbath, the seventh day that has no six? What shall we make of the irrelevance of men, the accentuations of racial tensions in its incidence and the intensifying threat of total dependence on a smaller and ever more subtle group of expert technocrats? Can life as we have known it survive, and can we survive not knowing it?

It is enough for our present purposes only to hint at these imponderables. That civilization seems to develop, in its contemporary form, the paradox of growing impersonality in the midst of, and as the price of, an increasing human attainment, underscores the whole theme on which we are embarked. The human privilege means, precisely, this responsibility for responsibility, the need and the capacity to preside, in conscious and inclusive authority, over the entire range of being human and to be radically confronted with issues that reach back from their partial sources into the whole significance of man. In a score of ways the meaning of the person in society seems to be jeopardized by developments within the relationship itself. Promise and prejudice seem to meet at the same point. It is in the very achievements of his current technology that man seems liable to forfeit the very secrets of himself. Alienation derives from the same factors that spell an external competence. The lack of the self appears to be the contradictory climax of the possessing of all things.

To raise these questions is in no way to be despairing: it is simply to repudiate the superficial optimism with which they can be minimized, and to keep the accent strenuously on both sides of the paradox. There are voices in some quarters making, so to speak, a virtue of the will to be sanguine and hailing the technological achievement as the *summum bonum*, and enthusiastically evading the inner miseries of men. Secularity then becomes the mature expression of liberation and the only proper 'gospel' of the time. The threat of impersonality in technocracy and cities has to be greeted as a sort of welcome relief from the ever present neighbour, and a correction, for which science may be thanked, of the undue relatedness of life, of man to man.[1] Exonerated by technology from many of the obligations, and some of the possibilities, of friendship and of old fashioned human-ness, we can approve the greater purposefulness of our own existence. There are perhaps aspects of these apostles of problemless good cheer needed to counter the novelists and poets of near despair to whom we turn in the next section. But we can hardly admit their thinking until justice has been done to the latter as being, plainly, the mirrors of our discontent. It is one thing to refuse the escapism of religion, and another to accept the escapism of secularity. The only way to honesty is through the dark tunnel of privation, even if some of its travellers have done no more than curse the darkness. This is the way which, with apologies to the Harvey Coxes and the William Hamiltons of our confident secular optimism, we propose to take.

CONTEMPORARY MAN: DISPOSSESSED OF HIMSELF

'A fever in matter' is one possible definition of life, and of all creatures only man would suggest it of or to himself. For as

[1] See, for example, Harvey Cox, *The Secular City*, New York, 1965, and the ingenious attempt to prefer to Buber's 'I and thou' personal encounter philosophy the remoter 'you' of the super-highway, the apartment building and the supermarket, where relatively impersonal dealings obtain.

Thomas Hobbes remarked in *Leviathan* 'absurdity is a privilege peculiar to man'.[1] It is odd that the arch villain of absolutism should employ our very own word! He was indeed accustomed to *le mot juste*. The sense of absurdity, the confession of it, even the mere fear of it, are certainly evidences of the dignity of men. 'I am and so I doubt not' could never be a reversal of Descartes' famous dictum, nor feasible for men.

At the close of Samuel Beckett's *Endgame*, Hamm observes: 'I was never there.' It seems clear that the novelist's purpose is really to say: 'No one has ever been there.' Extreme perhaps, but symptomatic of the desolating, yet somehow irreconcilable, loss of the self by the self, intimated with great skill in the very nebulousness of the atmosphere created by the story, where everything retreats into meaninglessness. Yet, perversely, it is a meaninglessness which seems to matter, if one is to judge from the passion and the violence with which it is portrayed. There seems no limit to the capacity for mistrust of things, no assurances—in this kind of literature—that can be relied upon. Hence it is that numbers of current writers are, so to speak, geriatricians of literature, preoccupied with old men, *Eh! Joe?* and *The Old Man and the Sea*. There is a chronic suspicion of plot and movement and action, so that the *mise-en-scène*, as in *Waiting for Godot*, has to be reduced to the barest severity of emptiness: 'a country road, a tree, evening', with no change save for the dubious and pathetic budding of the tree in the second act, which, like the rest of the intention, seems to subtract even while it adds, almost in a petulance of despair.

But if the literature of the lost self admits no significant progression of events, it also precludes all rational discourse. Eloquence, of course, is unthinkable: there must be no Shakespearean penetration of the grandeur of tragedy, no gentle kindliness in the perception of comedy. Conviction is self-disqualifying and even argument is suspect. Conversation, therefore, is reduced to a pointless, random sequence of inanities and no real debate emerges. For speech itself is phoney, since words deceive, whether in their conveyance of ideas or, more likely, by concealing the absence of

[1] Book I, Ch. V.

them. And, with the scepticism about all dialogue, goes a logical evacuation of character, and characters. The crowded panoramic scenes of Dickens, or of Tolstoy, or of Dostoevsky, give way to monotonous concentrations on a very few, or better even one *persona* whose very isolation repudiates the teeming world with all the plainer emphasis.

As thus reduced to its essential vacuity, the life of the anti-hero seems, in this kind of context, to imply that the very notion of identity is deceptive. Our search for certainty is itself perverse. Re-assurance will be always of necessity illusory, since it arises only from our need for self-importance. The only final 'value' would seem to be the capacity to avoid being fooled. Habit is here the arch-enemy, for it prevents us from really seeing the discontinuity in the flux of our experience, where honestly admitted, there is no enduring meaning and, indeed, no durable existence. The despair of this conclusion may be measured in the substitution of pointless mouthings, even digestive rumblings and bodily functions, for the sane and ordered sequences of rationality. The drift of soliloquy in, for example, Beckett's *Molloy* is pointedly pointless, chancing as it will, since nothing can ever be mentioned in its right place, yet in insistent subtle ways returning like a nagging fear to its listless pre-occupations.

Taking such literature, for the present, as a symptom of contemporary malaise, it would seem to combine a human inability to be nihilist with the inescapability of nihilism. *Waiting for Godot*, again, affords the readiest epitome of what, diversely, the mood intends to say. That single, central tree allows no shelter and focuses a great emptiness around it. If it is meant, in some sense, to have a cosmic reference and to hint at the Cross, the ambiguity and the deliberate attenuation seem to say confusedly that nothing can be looked for there. All is scruffy there. What goes on around this disreputable prop of despair is a kind of fable on negation. It stands as a permanent instrument of suicide as if to suggest the obvious solution. Yet it is never used. Life is, as it were, just the non-committing of suicide, with reason enough for the motive and none, discernibly, other than inertia, for the refusal of it. The two tramps are merely 'waiting'. Since they are waiting, there must be something they are waiting for. The something never appears. In their thwarted expectancy there is, therefore, a double negation: they can neither possess, nor abandon, their hope. They are caught in a folly of meaninglessness, made the more pathetic by their false but persistent dimension of expectancy. It is, in its broken way, a sort of negative study in Donne's familiar saying: *Qui fugit non effugit*. The only way to be human, it seems to say, is to renounce the effort, with the warning that neither effort nor renunciation can succeed. We are, in the end, no more than spectators of ourselves and unnecessary even so.

What are the sources of this attenuation of actuality thus reflected in these many writers, oscillating between melancholy and contempt? It is notable that the discounting of the self is all of one piece with a rejection of relation to environment, both natural and human. The loss of the self occurs in a desolation, either deliberate or inflicted, of the context in humanity. The degradation, in other words, is reciprocal. Man is inwardly disallowed where the context, in fact or in thought, is believed to disallow him. If man is displaced outside himself, he is alienated within himself but can neither escape nor tolerate the enmity. To exist, in the sense we have reviewed, with a minimal presence among others is to be a minimal self. The interior deprivation and the exterior degradation are one. Men cease to be, within themselves, because they cease to mean between themselves.

The reasons, either way, are complex and cumulative. There are, of course, the physical and mental futilities of war and occupation, of upheaval and distress.

Everything's asking us our opinions: *everything*. We're encircled by questions. The whole thing's a farce. Questions are asked as though we were men, as though somebody wanted us to believe that we still *are* men. It is a farce, this shadow of a question put by the shadow of a war to a handful of make-believe men . . .
Day after day we have got to gather in the rotten fruit of defeat, work out, in a world that's gone to pieces, that total choice I've just refused to

make ... He was conscious within himself of the panic fury of the trapped beast, and, looking up, saw the same fury in their eyes. Let them shout together to the far heavens: 'We've nothing to do with all this!'[1]

Such desperate exoneration presses in far more spheres than those of futile war. The world of 'peace' is even less amenable to significant enthusiasm or rides roughshod over the human search for relevance. American literature vividly reflects this fading of the dream, the disillusion which contrasts so sharply with the Jeffersonian optimism that went out, in hand with the Divine artificer, to conquer and subdue a continent. Conformism, banality, the stultification of ideals, the forfeiture of romance, ends reached and lost in the reaching—all these tend towards the atrophy of will and promote in writers either escapist fantasy or grim and sordid documentaries of decay.

Losing faith in their ability to restrict technological inventiveness to virtuous purposes, men have reacted violently; and in America, where the hostile or indifferent universe was always conquerable, especially by the innocent, the national experiment seems too far advanced to justify further anthems about its promise. Instead, the end-product is visible and hard to alter.[2]

Thus it is, that Ernest Hemingway, for example, finds his themes, for the most part, in the excitement of war and revolution and treats them with a vivid economy of style and terseness of graphic immediacy, saying aggressively enough: 'I was not made to think.' The only assurances here are those of the senses and these are to be cherished against the conspiracies of reality, as the only sure thing that life affords. Experience is not something that can be philosophically interpreted, or even arranged: what happens, as it happens, and with suitable rigour of style and sentiment, is all we can salvage from the emptiness of being.

There may be something appealing about his visual relation to

---

[1] Jean Paul Sartre, *Iron in the Soul*, trans. by Gerard Hopkins, 1963 edition, p. 56.

[2] Paul West, *The Modern Novel*, London, 1963, pp. 313-14.

environment but its essential distrustfulness of meaning is unmistakable. And there is a brutal thrust about its harshness.

I was always embarrassed by the words sacred, glorious and sacrifice ... We had heard them ... and had read them ... now for a long time, and I had seen nothing sacred, and the things that were glorious had no glory and the sacrifices were like the stockyards at Chicago if nothing was done with the meat except to bury it.[1]

Or Harry Morgan's dying summary of life:

He stopped. 'No matter how, a man alone ain't got no bloody chance.' He shut his eyes. It had taken him a long time to get it out and it had taken him all of his life to learn it.[2]

William Faulkner's world of Yoknapatawpha, the derelict south, with its stricken quality, its strife, ambition, neurosis, sordidness and sudden death, has a character subtly different from anything in Hemingway. But the logic is akin.

No battle is ever won, he said. They are not even fought. The field only reveals to man his own folly and despair, and victory is an illusion of philosophers and fools.[3]

Man is caught in 'a stalemate of dust and despair'.[4] Faulkner is an author who broods over a culture in decline, where avarice and cruelty abound, where lethargy and depravity aggravate each other. There are, from time to time, faint and enigmatic hints of redeemability, but they are deliberately oblique and, otherwise, there is neither clue nor remedy for the horror and insanity of life. Only 'the sound and the fury', 'signifying nothing'.

One need not opt for these morose or radical purveyors of the human contradictions, to take the corrosion of the time. It may be sensed in other form in the urbanity, for example, of E. M. Forster, whose villas and drawing rooms are worlds away from Spanish

---

[1] *A Farewell to Arms*, London, 1957, p. 130.

[2] *To Have and to Have Not*, London, 1954, p. 130.

[3] William Faulkner, *The Sound and the Fury*, New York, Vintage edition, 1946, p. 95.

[4] *Ibid.*, p. 143.

Wars and Jefferson, Mississippi. For him the world is unamenable to redemption or to final truth. Untidy and intractable to ideals, the world is best taken, as it were, by exemption. Let those who can, withdraw into secure areas of limited experience and let the rest survive or languish as they may. 'You and I and the Wilcoxes stand upon money as upon islands . . . most of the others are down below the surface of the sea.'[1] One cannot do otherwise without somehow 'believing in belief'—a luxury which mind cannot sustain or character afford. This opting out of any genuine humanity in the name of some secluded privacy of wealth, or indifference, or callous retreat, or exotic island remoteness, is familiar enough in twentieth-century writing. But always the repudiation of humanity around is the forfeiture of human-ness within, culminating in the Sartrean conclusion: 'Hell is other people.'

The factors within this alienation all belong, in close relation, with the present dimensions of man's dominion. Human inventiveness paradoxically jeopardizes the human meaning, creating or accentuating a human redundancy which deepens from purely economic or physical aspects into a threatening totality of irrelevance. The machine may heighten both the prestige and the cruciality of its experts: but it depreciates the worth and standing of the many. Or it tends to a dehumanizing of the processes by which it operates. The complexities of society readily argue an increasing pointlessness in the personal equation. The individual can all too easily capitulate to the conclusion that, whatever may be the forms of democracy, western or eastern, his own notions and verdicts are inconsequential. Or he is atrophied in the very will to 'mean' anything by the impression that the world around is dominated by forces, political and economic and financial, that have reduced him to futility.

This mitigation of the personal has, of course, a familiar ring and, though this is itself part of the problem, makes an almost banal observation by this time. What is more subtle and adverse is the deeper dubiety about the self from the notions of popular

[1] E. M. Forster, *Howards End*, New York, Vintage edition, 1954, p. 61.

psychology and the attrition of the very will to be, through the suspicion that it is illusory. It is not simply that the person is eliminated by the functionary in the technological world, but that man is also displaced within himself and is nevertheless unable, or is it simply unready?, to forgo his own consciousness and acquiesce in the anonymous self. There are those who argue that, both psychologically and sociologically, the old image of the independent self is outdated and overtaken. Just as the old forms of the anthropocentric attitude that turned on a geocentric belief about the universe have gone, so any form of anthropocentricity is now untenable and man must search for a kind of 'neutralized' or impersonal existence. This is the ironical conclusion drawn by many writers, and reflected in some of the despairers we have lately noted—ironical because it is, for these thinkers, the logical end-term of the most impressive achievements of the human intelligence. There are those who believe that somehow an impersonal personality can be viably attained and set about it by making a virtue of the necessity, as we have seen above, or by conceding defeat and conserving the bitterness, either plaintively or in defiance. To some aspects of this we will return in our discussion of 'bad faith' in Chapter VII. Or others take refuge in the sort of solution proffered by the drug manipulators, utilizing the possibilities of mental and psychological self-inducement, not for essentially restorative or ameliorative purposes within the self, but for its evacuation from reality.

For all these, belief in what used to be thought the real world is a form of romance. Hence the vehement anti-hero, the barren anti-literature, we have discussed. The 'disenchantment' which so many have urged upon us, in the sense of treating nature with cold scientific detachment and no Wordsworthian emotions 'charged with grandeur', has now penetrated to the inner self. The sequence might have been expected, since the self is inevitably devalued that devalues its relationships. Authenticity, like peace, is indivisible. Man is likely to disappear from art (the anti-drama, the anti-picture), when art, that is wonder, disappears from nature, This means, also, in the end, a sort of anti-science too—not in the sense merely of a scientific acceptance of inconsistency (for this is a growing necessity within its logic), but in the sense of a repudiation of the wholeness of the scientist himself, as being not merely a specialist with an equation or a discovery, but a part in a social whole, a participant in a historical process and a neighbour among his fellows. We cannot abstract the scientific procedures from the general world or pretend somehow that the world stops at the laboratory door or is not there when it is re-opened. Whatever the limitations of Teilhard de Chardin's writings technically,[1] it is their supreme merit to have insisted with courage and imagination on the entire context of the scientific venture and its over-all relatedness, and it is just this which scientists rooted in their specialisms have too often willed to ignore. From that neglect has come attrition of the human whole which now masquerades, in some quarters, as a new realism. The ultimate logic of the scientific enterprise is in fact to demonstrate that specialism is impossible, except as a necessary methodology of concentration—impossible because the fruits of its very achievements return men more and more to the whole and make ever more total and inescapable the responsibility to be responsible. This must mean, in the end, the restoration of the true romantic, sobered, it is true, and disciplined, but not essentially denied. A science of irresponsibility, like a literature of despair, is plainly a contradiction in terms. If those who argue acquiescence in the loss of selfhood in the name of realism only took the status of their disquiet seriously enough it would lead them back to confidence. Despair about man within man can only be authentic as a sign of salvation. For if it were true in any other context, it could not arise. Camus may serve us in this conclusion in Chapter VII. The point here meanwhile is that the things which most threaten the meaning of man form the crux of the possession of it. The anti-romantic is the least realist of all.

That, however, is plainly a conviction which cannot be imposed. It can only be embraced. The point in exploring, through

[1] See, for example, the angry, technical discussion in P. B. Medawar, *The Art of the Soluble*, London, 1967, pp. 71–81, which, for all its incisiveness, misses the real point.

the chapters that follow, an ancient Semitic assurance about the double quality of human existence as at once an empire and a reverence, is to discover its secret for our own so different time. It calls us neither to disown the competence nor to forsake the worship. It declares that there is no escape in fear and less in arrogance. We must accept the mastery and yet intensify the adoration. By its light the human situation is an act of faith made in us and so received by us. And this is the reason why, if it is not taken as sacred, it has to be indicated as absurd. For unless it is a trust, it is certainly a mockery. To find it intolerable as the latter— as all despair does—is the negative corroboration of its status as the former. Man is the condition of all values because they have been rooted in his response. This gives him at once both mastery and subordination: he is defining and defined within the real, achiever and achieved. The trust by which he commands is the stature in which he is tributary. *Servare est regnare: regnare est servare.*

Our sense of alienation, then, in the midst of possession has to be taken into its deepest relevance, not as a counsel of rejection, but a measure of vocation. It comes only because, over against a *whole* world of significance, we have forgotten our humility, or in a partial world of value we have been misled by our pretension. In either case, we have been entrusted and, refusing the trust in pride or in fear, have found intolerable that which only worship and courage, in their partnership, can properly sustain. What then we take for the disproof of meaning, the irony of the absurd, is none other than the consistency of the covenant by which we are constituted. The fact, therefore, that history should have sharpened the inward crisis where it has intensified the outward sovereignty is no surprise. For every accentuating enlargement of the effective stature of man surely means a deepened expression of his essential being and a larger test of its will to decision. If the old Biblical and Quranic accounts of man, studied in the sequel, do no more than focus the central fact of that crisis, apart altogether from the acceptance of their total faith, the venture will be justified.

For it will be at least a venture in realism, abjuring the partial-izing of existence which is practised by a piety remote from power, or a science oblivious of society and the transcendent. For it is the fallacy of empirical science to 'offer as a safe harbour what is the ocean itself, the storms, the waves, the shipwrecks, namely man's experience of himself and the "objective" world'.[1] We cannot rightly rely, however easy the temptation, on the procedures of the technological realm as if the sheer pursuit of them or some convenient neglect of their repercussions in every other realm of life could take care of the total situation in which they are merely a part. Nor should the whole be dismissed as if it were a foolish pre-occupation contrasting ill with the efficiencies of a scientific analysis, as for example in the sardonic aloofness of Medawar: 'The Predicament of Man is all the rage now that people have sufficient leisure and are sufficiently well-fed to contemplate it and many a tidy literary reputation has been built upon exploiting it.'[2] Such sentiments are libellous of past ages and quite superficial in their arrogance. 'The anguish of being' is more than such urbanity has understood and is not to be bowed out as an uncouth intruder in some royal society or an inconvenient ghost disturb-ing a laboratory. We do not face man by disdaining his fears or mistaking his sciences as his pride only and not also his distress.

But this duty in no way means a contrasted refuge in timidity and evasive religion, whether perverse or passive. Nor does it argue some recession to a past devotion, or any archaism of the soul, nor yet a venture in the imitation of older and serener faith. Rather, if we may borrow from Erich Heller a graphic imagina-tion, itself kindled by the grim and thrusting honesties of Vincent Van Gogh, we are content to read the holy in the lowliest form and to find the word where we meet the flesh. 'He painted . . . the boots that are the chance receptacles of all the homeless energy of the spirit which once had its lawful house with Giotto's

---

[1] See Erich Heller, *The Disinherited Mind*, London, 1961 edition, p. 232.

[2] *Op. cit.*, p. 80. This over-all dismissal of De Chardin gives the sensitive reader pause even over Medawar's legitimate criticisms.

angels and madonnas—once a king in kingdoms, now a squatter in boots.'[1]

Either way, and whatever the time, it is one theme—man and his going out, his coming in, the high places and the lowly, the kingdom to gain and the kingdom to lay down, the power and the glory, the dominion received and the dominion rendered.

[1] *Op. cit.*, p. 243.

II

'God is, and Man is His Caliph':
A Quranic View

'DOMINION status' is a term with a lengthening history in British constitutional law. But its origins are neither legal nor political and have nothing to do with inter-imperial relationships and the Statute of Westminster. They are Biblical and theological and concern an interchangeable concept of God and man. 'Bless the Lord all his works in all places of his dominion' says Psalm ciii in its final summons to adoration. 'Thou madest him to have dominion over the works of thy hands' declares Psalm viii in celebrating the dignity of man. If the word 'dominion' with its Latin echoes seemed apt to twentieth-century jurists concerned for powers in relation, it only lay to hand because seventeenth-century translators had used it, with evident relish, to describe the Biblical stature of humanity as feasibly exercising an authority akin to God's.

It is nearly, if not precisely, this notion of the 'dominion' of man which is denoted in the Quranic term *khalīfah*. The purpose of this Chapter is to explore the usage in the Qur'ān, to relate it to the Judeo-Christian parallel, and to consider its liberating and hallowing significance against the background of the contemporary human paradox of increasing competence and decreasing assurance just reviewed. How does the human status, as Islamically understood, illuminate and interpret that strange possession in dispossession, that exploiting authority and exploited contradiction, of the human which the modern scene discloses in its mingled pathos and achievement?

The definitive passage in the Qur'ān is Surah 2. 30. 'Thy Lord said to the angels: "I am appointing a viceroy in the earth."' The angels at once demur at this announcement, drawing pained attention to their peaceableness and perpetual adoration as contrasted with the fickle, blood-shedding pugnacity of men for whom this dignity of viceregality is proposed. The Divine response is, in effect, that God keeps his own counsel and proceeds upon surer, deeper knowledge. The text continues with an account of man's being taught the names of things—always a Semitic image for sovereignty and anticipating the vital role of nomenclature in the processes of science. This human competence in identifying, naming, and so managing, phenomena is something the angels have to confess they cannot match or attain. Thus effectively silenced as to their complaint, the angels are called upon to 'worship' Adam, the archetypal man. The imperative verb here may be translated 'prostrate before' him, if one wishes to avoid the implication that anything more than a symbolic acknowledgement is meant. The fact, however, remains that the verb is the one otherwise invariably used for the human recognition of the Divine worth. It would, therefore, seem more loyal to the import of the passage to take it as indicating that the Divine lordship itself is in some sense staked in the human role, that the due recognition of humanness is inseparable from the proper, angelic acknowledgement of God. At all events, man's dignity stands through Divine counsels: to contest the one is to decry the other.

Such a conclusion is certainly the logic of what follows. For *Iblīs*, the Devil, refuses to bow before man. His defiance of God takes the form of a denial of man: it is in rejecting the status with which the creature is endowed that *Iblīs* repudiates the Creator's authority. There could hardly be, in terms of myth and symbol, a clearer affirmation of the lordship of man as that which may not be spurned without impugning the sovereignty of God. The celestial insurrection, if we may put it this way, turns on a terrestrial issue: God is flouted where man is despised. Or, in positive terms, Adam is, so to speak, the test and crux of the Divine will and wisdom.

There are other Quranic passages which deal with the recalcitrance of Satan at the creation of man,[1] but Surah 2. 30 is the only

---

[1] See Surah 7. 10–17 and 15. 26–40. Here the subsequent temptation of man

occurrence in the Qur'ān of the singular word *khalīfah*, save for
Surah 38. 26 where it is found in a Divine address to David: 'O
David, We have appointed you a viceroy in the earth: judge
rightly between men and do not be beguiled by desire.' Though,
following many commentators, this verse may be interpreted
politically, this is by no means a necessary, or an exclusive
exegesis, and there is in any event no sense of an established
succession. Power and trusteeship are the essential ideas in this
royal address and they relate closely to the same twin themes of
Adam's calling under God.

Plural uses of this term in the Qur'ān will be noted below.
They corroborate the point which it is important here to stress,
namely that the Quranic 'caliphate' is not the political institution
later developed to serve the continuity of Muḥammad's achievement after his death, but the general dominion of Adam in the
world.[1] The historic Caliphate no doubt borrows and takes over
the implicit idea and, appropriately to the whole instinct of
Islam, gives it a political perpetuation. But without in any way
detracting from the obvious centrality to Islamic history of that
Caliphal succession, it is well to insist that as far as the text of the
Qur'ān is concerned the 'imperium' with which we have to do is
that which belongs to man, and that the vicegerency he exercises
is on behalf of God. There can be no question that 'Alī 'Abd
al-Rāziq was right in his emphasis in 1925, shortly after the final
demise of the Caliphate at the hands of Atatürk, that it had been a
de facto creation of the Arab genius, authentic and vital through
long centuries but nevertheless lacking any explicit Quranic basis.
For that perspective helps to bring into unclouded prominence

by the Devil is designed to demonstrate how right the Devil is, by making plain
how fickle, unreliable, rebellious and unworthy is the creature God has rashly
dignified with the rule of earth.

[1] This truth makes it the more strange to read in so perceptive an authority as
E. I. J. Rosenthal, in *Political Thought in Medieval Islam*, Cambridge, 1958, p. 26,
the view that 'the Caliphate as an institution is based on the Qur'ān'. After
quoting the two passages noted, he adds: 'The nature of the Caliph is clearly
defined here: he is the vicegerent of Muḥammad ... thus he commands spiritual
authority and is at the same time temporal ruler and judge.'

the deeper concern of the Qur'ān for the inclusive 'caliphate' of man himself.[1]

The political focus of the human 'empire', the assumption, by state power, of its operative expression and control, are no doubt justifiable and logical. But in the meaning of the Adamic 'caliphate' those civil, legal or military embodiments of dominion are strictly tributary to the proper responsibility of men as men for the custody of the good earth, and to their whole engagement with the natural order in its economic, social and spiritual significance. It is because 'the earth is the Lord's' in Islamic doctrine, as well as in Hebrew psalmody, that all political sovereignty has to be seen as instrumental to the Divine purpose. Man, generic man, man in Adam before his racial, ethnic or material contentions and divergencies, is the crux of both. The state has to be finally accountable to human stature and subservient to human ends, because this human 'reference' of its powers and duties is the touchstone of its service to the Divine lordship. Political power is not rightly tributary to God if it is falsely exploitative or oppressive of men. For behind its external and effective sanctions lie the dignities of common men in the keeping of the sovereignty of God.

It is for this reason that there is more than a simple error of exegesis in the view that mistakenly assumes that political rule in succession to the Prophet is the sense of the *khilāfah*, or vicegerency, of Adam. Indeed, only when its proper, authentic meaning as denoting the human order deriving from the archetypal man is acknowledged, can there be any legitimacy in the institutional, political organ to which commentary has applied it. It is a perversion to regard the Islamic privilege of man as somehow capable of being interpreted, still less achieved, in this external, political expression.[2] Justice to the Quranic intention in

[1] In his radical study *Islam and the Sources of Authority* (Al-Islām wa Uṣūl al-Ḥukm), Cairo, 1925.

[2] This was the main thrust of 'Alī 'Abd al-Rāziq's study. Though something of a *tour de force* at the time of its publication, its arguments have now been widely agreed. We still urgently need his emphasis that continuity in Islam has, and can have, no external guarantee in any form of government, but only in living conformity to its meaning.

this regard is now, of course, more readily done in that the historic Caliphate no longer exists to obscure the term or exclusify the meaning.

To turn to the plural uses of *khalīfah* in the Qur'ān is to find these reflections confirmed. *Khalā'if* occurs on several occasions but always with the general sense of temporal successiveness and thus of replacement. Thus Surah 10. 14: 'After them We set you as viceroys in the earth in order to see how you would react.' Here, in a characteristic emphasis, the Qur'ān records the mission of God's prophets and messengers and the awesome flux of history, with disobedient generations passing away, to be succeeded by others who are to take sombre warning from the retributions of history. 'Taking the room of' is throughout the initial sense of the verb *khalafa*, but always with the accompanying ideas of either 'following after' and/or 'occupying in lieu of'. The second meaning is necessarily detached from 'succession' in all that has to do with God. The Eternal is never superseded but He may entrust His will to deputies on His behalf. The two meanings of the verb, as it were, morally substantiate each other. For the Qur'ān sees the fact of generations, in their sequence, as a constant reminder of the fact of accountability. Time's transitoriness is also its reckoning. Men on both counts are no more than tenants. *Pereunt et imputantur.*

In Surah 10. 73 Noah and his company, emerging from the ark are 'appointed viceroys' in the recovered earth—again the double idea of replacement and responsibility. It is not a continuity of rulers that is in mind but the moral sequences of requital and renewal. Again in 35. 39 the reader finds the same context of ethical duty and warning. God discerns the innermost thoughts. Surah 6. 165 has the same words and adds that the 'viceroys' are differentiated in rank or endowment 'that He may put you to the test in His gifts'. All, it may be noted, are alike in their status, though differing in their quality. As the preceding verses insist, the dignity is inalienable and there are no proxies in the reckoning. In similar vein, Surah 7. 69 (using the alternative plural *khulafā'*) specifies the building of castles and the mining of hills as typical

works of man's occupancy in time and place and bids these
denizens of earth preserve their sojourn from corrupting deeds.

It is perhaps worth noting that the term *ista'marakum*: 'He has
planted you as tenants . . .' occurring in similar contexts, derives
from a prolific Arabic root which combines the same twin ideas
of time-tenancy and place-tenancy and yields terms for a span of
years and for an abode, a dwelling, an establishment. 'Long and
prosperous' are readily conjoined in many languages, insofar as
time and room are a condition, if by no means a guarantee, of
success. Men in this sense are all empire builders, exploiting the
occasions of the years and of the lands, and all by the Divine
design and leave. It is strange how that final English word
captures the identical notion, holding in one both permission and
departure. Men have ends and an end: they are lease-holders in
the world. Whatever their success, it is shadowed by succession.
Their competence is bounded by their mortality. From both they
derive their standing as common imperialists, ploughing, sowing,
planting, reaping, building, acquiring, using, consuming and
being consumed. This is their caliphate, over things and unto
God.

The minor prophet, Ṣāliḥ, who expresses this theme of 'empire'
in 11. 61 adds, significantly 'so ask of Him forgiveness'. The
sequence of thought is in line with the constant re-iteration in the
Qur'ān of the obligation on the part of men to a recognition of
the hallowedness of the material world. The terrestrial occupancy
which man enjoys must not be vulgarized by casual or possessive
attitudes which ignore or despise the postures of prayer and
gratitude. It can only be as a worshipper Godward that man
rightly takes and pursues his physical empire. It is for this reason
that the need to be forgiven is, Quranically, never far from the
claim or the capacity to exploit. The sense that this is so is the
inner experience of the dominion status. Precisely because man is
caliph over nature he is aware, through the instincts of awe and
the word of revelation, of this spiritual, one might almost say,
poetic, dimension of his 'science'.

Hence, of course, the steady Quranic call to grateful wonder and reverence. *La'alla* runs like a refrain through scores of appeals and pleas—'the grand perhaps' of the Qur'ān's expectation of the human response. 'Perhaps you may give thanks', 'perhaps you may come to your senses', 'perhaps you may ponder and con- sider'—the phrases recur with impressive urgency, evoking the sort of cognisance of the external world that is proper to intelli- gent and thankful persons mindful of the dependable mysteries in the midst of which they move, whether of farms and oases, of sex and pregnancy, of wind and sun, of death and life. Nature has to be seen, by these criteria, as a sacramental realm in which phenomena indicate, or better intimate, a meaning that is more than their mere physical occurrence.

Always, in this context there is the kinship of recognition and significance. A sense of the relevance of things marches with the attentiveness with which they are noted and observed. The two combine in the parallel Quranic notion of 'signs'. These *āyāt* are present throughout human experience in the context of nature and in the events of life. What happens on the physical or natural plane—harvest, a childbirth, a wellspring, sexual exchanges in marriage, even wind propulsion in ships at sail—are all esteemed as foci of a mercy, or a purposefulness, which are more than their factual quality as phenomena and take the perceptive spirit into reaches of delight and wistful wonder unknown to the merely brazen or the negligent.

It has become almost traditional for modern Muslim thought to find in the Quranic theme of the 'signs' in nature a whole philosophy of scientific attitudes. Here, it is said, is the character- istic assumption of empirical science, namely that nature must be taken as a realm of intelligibility waiting to be explored and 'organized' by the observational disciplines that science pursues. There is no need for outside assessments to quarrel with this line of exegesis. In one sense Scriptures are what their adherents take them to be: their meanings are what their learners receive from them. True, the Quranic posture of attentive recognition towards the natural order is essentially a religious attitude, and there is undoubted anachronism in reading into it the assumptions or instincts of the modern scientific mind. Nevertheless, there is arguably a legitimate development from the one to the other. Just as the medieval European theological confidence in the rationality of experience provided the matrix of modern science, so the fundamentally religious demand of Islam that nature be seen and received as 'significant' may properly be claimed as a foreshowing and a parable of the necessary commitment of scientific activity to the tasks of experimental observation and the duties of attentive evaluation. For all science, in its relation to its themes and objects, is in this broad sense *muslim*, that is, submissive, subduing its activity to the givenness, the data, of that with which it is engaged. To that extent the scientific and the religious are not essentially remote from each other, or mutually exclusive. On the contrary, the Quranic and religious assurance that human experience holds secrets none but the reverent learn has an evidently close relation to the scientific, modern conviction by which experiment and induction proceed. To avow this is in no way, of course, to imply that when Muḥammad's first Meccan and Medinan hearers received the Qur'ān they heard or heeded any call to become laboratory technicians. The excesses of eager exegesis must not detract from the inherent potential of kindred ideas. The impulses of a deferential science move readily with and through a religious awareness of the natural realm. It is to this the *āyāt*, or 'signs', of the Qur'ān call every successive generation, in what we must see as the cumulative, yet common, caliphate of mankind through them all.

Shukr, or gratitude, and *tafakkur*, or alertness to the *āyāt*, are, at all events, factors in the right temper of 'dominion status'. They clearly belong with the double vocation to mastery and to worship which constitutes man as the *khalīfah* or viceroy. The sustained emphasis they receive in the Quranic doctrine of the human standing is to be understood as the claim that dignity makes and the due condition of its exercise.

All the foregoing is corroborated if we revert briefly to the Satanic cavilling at the creation and authority of man which we noted in Surahs 2, 7 and 15. We saw the 'spite' of *Iblīs* as determined at all costs to prove its grudge, by demonstrating the quick corruptibility of the new creature. Had not part of the angelic apprehension about man been 'that he would go to bad' in it and with it? The term here is a recurrent one, namely *tufsidu fīhā*, i.e. 'deal corruptly' or 'do evil', and expresses that perpetual foreboding about the risk of the human experiment that is the other side of the Qur'ān's deep sense of the seriousness of existence. Satan, at least, is persuaded that God has miscalculated and is out to make the point as sharply and as soon as may be. Nor does even the scantiest attention to history suggest that he would ever have had much difficulty. Rather any realistic contemplation of the human scene must evoke the conjecture as to whether the human business was not an ill-starred venture. Any honesty about man must involve a dark misgiving about his 'justification', given the endless, tragic stretches of waste and folly and wrong with which his story is defiled.

And so it is that the Devil's charge about Divine misconceiving and miscalculation gathers into a single, mythical 'accusation' of man in the utmost and elemental sense, man not merely as 'the mistake of creation'[1] as D. H. Lawrence has it, but man as the crime of creation. The Satanic enmity to man amounts to a sort of prosecution of God in respect of man, a kind of inclusive disavowal of the Divine wisdom in the avowal of the human futility. We have, thus, in mythical form the whole 'desirability' of man challenged and decried. *Iblīs* is, therefore, the 'accuser', the 'enemy' whose articulate malevolence, far from being an academic aloofness, impels and goads him to a deliberate, urgent undoing of the human meaning.

This would seem to be the ultimate sense lying behind the Islamic term *al-Shaiṭān al-rajīm*, 'the accursed Satan', which occurs four times in the Qur'ān[2] and may be linked with the psalmist's

---

[1] In *Women in Love*, London, 1921, p. 102, where Birkin remarks: 'There would be no absolute loss if every human being perished tomorrow ... Do you find it a beautiful, clean thought, a world empty of people, just uninterrupted grass and a hare sitting up? Man is ... the mistake of creation.'

[2] Surahs 3. 36; 15. 17; 16. 98; 81. 25.

phrase about 'the enemy',[1] in a passage to which we will turn later. The Arabic root R J M, from which *rajīm* derives, means 'to stone', or 'to curse' and 'revile'. The 'stoning' of Satan in the pilgrimage rites symbolizes the utter repudiation of his ways and his wiles. But this physical meaning of the term arises, or so it may be argued, from a sort of reflexive situation, in which the 'being stoned' by men answers to Satan's scornful rejection of man. This then gives an active sense to the adjective, approximating with surprising closeness to the Greek term *diabolos*, that is, the slanderer and the adversary, who in Biblical contexts in both Testaments is 'the accuser' of the brethren.[2]

The first of the last two Surahs of the Qur'ān, familiarly known as 'the refuge-seekers', lists among its fears 'the evil of the envier when he envies'—an apprehension which has sometimes been taken to refer to the threatening contumacy of Satan. This is echoed in 23. 98: 'O my Lord, I take refuge with Thee from the evil suggestions of the Satans.' These and other references may relate to alternative aspects of demonic hostility to men, including the deception which misguides the reciter in his reading of the sacred text (Surah 16. 98). But this general import has certainly to do with that antipathy of which the creation narrative speaks. It seems right, therefore, especially if one can be fortified by Biblical associations, to see the ultimate reach of that anti-human malice as a malevolence kindled by the evident status and the arguable folly of the creature. In the odd, but apt, phrase it is 'the Devil's advocacy' of the Devil himself, a giving of the lie to the very creativity of God expressed in the nature and stature of men. In this light, it is not hard to detect the intention of the psalmist when he sings that 'out of the mouth of babes and sucklings' is 'praise perfected', whereby 'to still the enemy and the avenger'. For every new child is a renewal of the human opportunity, each fresh generation a new and potential recurrence of man, a further embodiment of the Divine expectation towards the human spirit, a new occasion of the created destiny. The newness may not of

---

[1] Ps. viii. 2.
[2] Rev. 12. 10 and Job 1. 6 and 9 *et al.*

itself arrest the bias of the generations before. But, despite that entail, the child is the pledge that 'God has not wearied of mankind'.

Some commentators on the psalm, it is true, see 'the enemy' as the old chaos, resistant to creative power, or the inertia which the Divine will had to overcome in fashioning the world. But even then the attribution of the crucial quelling of 'the enemy' to the efficacy of 'praise' might be taken to suggest that worship, readiest from within the simplicities of the child spirit, most surely disarms man's rebellion and so belies the malicious discredit with which Satan wilfully maligns the creature.

It will be cautious not to press too strongly on the Quranic sense of 'the accursed Devil' these Biblical parallels. Yet there is more than a hint of kinship with them in the eloquent opening of Surah 67:

Blessed be He in whose hand is the Kingdom, the all powerful One, who created death and life, that He might put you to test and know the worthiest in deed among you, He the strong and the forgiving, Who created in order the seven heavens. You will not find any imperfection in the handiwork of the all merciful. Scan it carefully anew: can you note any flaw? Look yet again, and again, and your gaze is dazzled and wearied.

Then follows the remarkable comment: 'We adorned the lower heaven with lamps and made them to serve for the stoning of Satans.' 'Missiles for pelting devils' runs one translation, too crudely. Can the passage not be set within the dimensions of our earlier analysis, so that the very majesty of the universe flings back upon the cavillers against man the lies in their own perversity? We have not begun to apprehend the splendour of being if we turn from the contemplation of the universe in either calumny or despair.

That insistence, however, whatever may be finally decided here exegetically, only makes more crucial the trusteeship, in that universe, of the human custodians. There can be no re-asserting the goodness of existence, over against the animosity of demonic 'accusation', without returning imperatively to the responsibility of man. Every acceptance of the mystery and desirability of the world 'puts to test', as the Qur'ān insists, the temper and trust-ability of humanity, and this, precisely, is what their 'caliphate' is about. Those awesome heavens and planetary fidelities of Surah 67 silence every jealous whisper against the wisdom of creation only by awaiting, in that silent splendour, the answer of the human crisis.

Another remarkable, if enigmatic, passage in the Qur'ān is brought to mind by this conclusion. In Surah 33. 72, 'the trust' of God is offered to the heavens and the earth. When these, out of awe, refused to take it, man 'bore it'. What the skies and hills declined, man, to translate freely, 'proved wilfully wrong' in the way he took over. There are three significant terms here which would seem to hold the clue to the intention of this intriguing verse, namely al-amānah, 'the trust'; ẓalūman, 'sinful' or, one might even venture 'outrageous'; and jahūlan, 'ignorant', with an implication of 'stubbornness'.

What is this amānah? 'We proposed the faith' runs Sale's version. 'Trust' is very generally preferred by most English renderings. Is there a suggestion of some primordial 'reason' in the heavens and in the hills, some capacity for reflective thought and decision? Or could this be, as it were, a hypothecation of a human parallel, implying that had the non-sentient world been confronted with the opportunity of the status man enjoys, it would in awe and wonder have begged to be allowed to forego so high a dignity? If so, the text becomes a deeply suggestive emphasis on the conscious authority of man. The sense, therefore, would seem to reach back into that varied meaning of islām itself (as a common noun denoting acceptance of obligation) which several modern Muslim writers have explored. Can it be said, for example, that there is an islām of planets and of atoms, of stars and molecules, in that their behaviour is expressible in 'laws' which they fulfil? If so, such islām is clearly 'necessary' and non-volitional and, being so, is not strictly describable as islām, if that term is properly to be reserved for the conscious, willing, free and, therefore, optional, surrender of man to the 'laws' of his true being. While, accordingly, there is some point in seeing the whole universe as *muslim*, or 'conforming to law', it is proper to identify the true, discerning, responsible *islām* in man alone.

This, it would appear, is what Surah 33. 72, in its figurative way, is saying. The elemental world truly 'obeys' but it does not possess 'option'. Or, rather, in terms of the passage, its 'option' is to have no option. Only man takes, in deliberate capacities of will and choice, the burden of metaphysical awareness and, by the same token, the burden of existence. In so taking, he places himself under the obligations of his creaturehood but is so con- stituted that these will hinge, only and always, upon his inner determination. Truly the range of his competent 'election' for this or that, against that or this, is not limitless. He is plainly encompassed with circumstance and frailty. Nevertheless, these conditions only undergird, and never withhold, the ultimate 'optionability' that uniquely characterizes the human status.

Man, then, is Promethean in the sense that he enjoys aptitudes and engages in ventures, elsewhere precluded, though not, as we shall see below, Promethean in the sense that these powers, this privilege, is wrung from a reluctant heaven and only perpetuated by a kind of desperate defiance. Quite the contrary. It is *amānah*, entrustment, anticipating trustworthiness. Man's abilities are seen as the other side of a Divine expectation, his occasions are a steady encounter with vocation.

Here, precisely, is the point, the tragedy, of *ẓalūman* and *jahūlan*. The two adjectives derive from crucial and fertile roots in Quranic Arabic and some of their implications will recur below in Chapter V. The former belongs with that central con- cept of *ẓulm* and the latter with the *Jāhiliyyah* that characterized the days before Islam. The meaning here is that man's exercise of the trust of the world errs, violates, distorts, wrongs and blunders. It is at once exploitative and foolish, injurious and wayward, wrongful and stupid. The terms present in fact an inclusive amalgam of the accumulated injustice and folly of humanity in history. The ignorance in *jahūlan* is not merely witless, it is obstinate: the evil in *ẓalūman* is not simply adverse, it is wilful. Together the words comprise the sort of indictment Satan had already, in anticipation, levelled against the counsels in heaven about the creation of man. Yet the *amānah* continues, the counsels stand, the experiment persists, the race renews its generations, history accumulates and the heavens and the hills maintain their steady, dependable neutrality for man and about him. The physical world, says Surah 33. 72, in its prescient way, feared: man did not fear and the world fears yet more.

This, then, is the Quranic caliphate—not some political institution, organized in single rulers to perpetuate Muḥammad's legacy, but the whole, universal, plural dignity of all men, as men, in their empire over things and under God. The two prepositions are, clearly, inter-dependent. Man has no sovereignty *over* the world, except in accountability *under* God. He cannot enjoy the relativities of race, nation, power, possessions, if he absolutizes either their claims or their pursuit. Contrariwise, he does not truly acknowledge the Divine except in the concreteness of his responsible authority. He needs, if we may move into New Testament terminology, his status as a 'king' if he is to be effectively a 'priest'. His only 'royalty' is sacramentally tributary beyond himself: his only 'priesthood' is, not some abstracted piety, some ritual convention, but the sure hallowing of his whole 'imperium'. The idea in the term *khalīfah* incorporates both these directions of his being. It proclaims man as by Muslim prayer symbolized, a being at once properly erect and properly prostrate, commanding and commanded.[1]

That we are not, in this reading, isolating a single notion, and a few passages, of the Qur'ān improperly to sustain a case it should not bear, can be demonstrated from several other strands within it. Take, for example, the confidence of Surahs 21. 16 and 44. 38

---

[1] It may perhaps be right to note that N. A. Faris in *The Muslim World*, Vol. 24, 1934, pp. 183–6, makes the ingenious suggestion that in Surah 2. 30 one should read *khalīqah* for *khalīfah* (one diacritical point difference), meaning 'creature' not 'caliph'. But aside from the textual impediments to such a proceeding, the whole onus of the argument would seem to be obscured or excluded.

that God has 'not created the heaven (in the second passage: the heavens) and the earth in jest'. 'Had it been Our will to indulge in jest, We would have found it', adds the former text, 'within Our Presence, had such been the sort of thing We do.' The implication, clearly, is that man is not a laughing matter, not a sport of heaven: the creation is not an enterprise in cruel mockery. Commenting on the point, the classic commentator, Al-Baiḍāwī, says: 'Rather We created them (i.e. the heavens and the earth) freighted with all kinds of wonders to arrest the attention of the beholder, and as a token to the intelligent, and as a means whereby the affairs of the servants of God may be ordered in this life and in the life to come.' Man can, he adds, 'climb thus to the attainment of perfection'. Or, in other terms, the caliphal quality of man, his actual and his potential empire, is assured in the processes by which the natural order yields, in dependable constancy, to his curiosity and his control. Under the aegis of a Divine integrity, discernible in the fidelities by which 'knowledge becomes power', man moves freely within the world and finds a dominion which does not play him false.[1]

In the same vein, it would seem, the reader may take the early verses of Surah 55, perhaps the most celebrated of all 'nature' passages in the Qur'ān, with its refrain: 'O which of your Lord's bounties will you and you deny?' God, run the verses in question, 'created man and taught him *al-bayān*'. How should the last word be rendered? 'The clue' might be the most fitting answer. Arberry has 'the Explanation', Pickthall 'utterance', and Abu-l'Fazl 'clear speech'. The underlying idea is that of apprehension and expression, the making articulate of that which has become plain. It is natural that the term should have been frequently taken to mean the Qur'ān itself and it is so employed in Surah 3. 138. Certainly in 'reading' the Qur'ān[2] the believer is at once learning and affirming the meaning: *al-bayān* is 'the manifesting' both as inward awareness and outward communication. But in 55. 4

---

[1] 44. 39 would seem to uphold this line of exegesis: 'We created them not save with truth'.

[2] The term *Al-Qur'ān* means, of course, 'reading' or 'recital'.

there would seem to be a broader sense of the term, applicable
to the human cognisance of external nature and man's interpreting
realization of his whole environment. There might even be, in
that sense, a sort of parallel between 'reciting' the Scripture and
discerning the world. Adam, as we saw, was taught the names of
things and was thus related intelligently to an intelligible creation.
The resulting wisdom, speaking, as it were, the grammar of the
natural order, was the *bayān*, or understanding, which he owed
to the Divine tuition.

It seems right to venture, in this way, a rough parallel between
the reception of the Qur'ān and the perusal of the world. The pen,
in either case, is needed for the recording of meaning and, thus,
in turn, for its further accessibility as knowledge or as Scripture.
The Qur'ān is much interested in this 'use of the pen'.[1] Truly,
the strictly revelatory content of the Book corrects, enlarges,
corroborates, guides and over-rules this natural knowledge. But
it does not displace or despise it. Man, therefore, is given *al-bayān*,
a communicable discernment of his environment. This, enjoyed
and exchanged among men, is the instrument of the responsible
caliphate which is man's creaturely prerogative.

The foregoing suffices to set in focus the Islamic account of the
human privilege implicit in the term *khalīfah*, as the Qur'ān
employs it. It coincides broadly with the Biblical dominion. To
be sure, the thought of 'the image of God', so pivotal in the
Hebrew tradition, does not figure explicitly in Quranic vocabulary. 'After Our likeness' is language which Islam instinctively
avoids. Yet insofar as that *imago Dei* concept is fulfilled in this
awareness of man as having creativity within nature and a
dominion for God's sake, the absence of the term and the silence
about its other Biblical significance need not be over drawn.
Much of the intention of the phrase is already here. In effect the
caliphate of the Qur'ān *is* the dominion of the Bible: in practical
senses the larger, bolder terminology of Genesis may be said to
be implied. Mastery and control in due subordinate order within

---

[1] Surahs 68. 1 and 96. 4.

the Divine will are the essential quality of 'man made in the image of God'. God, in that sense, affords an analogy for man. The 'likeness' concerns a lordship and the role by which man fulfills it, within the non-human world, gives that world a new relation to God Himself. The ploughman, for example, in the creation serves ends that the creation itself, and thus, surely, the God of creation, expect and intend. Husbandry, indeed, makes good the creation by rendering the partnerships it ordains. The same must be understood about all the technological elaborations of that possessiveness and exploitation of which husbandry is the most elemental form. The place left for man in the scheme of things is seen to be a vicegerency, where the feasibility of conquest and control is discovered to be a delegated trust.

If, without strain, we can in this way link the Quranic Adam with the Biblical in a comparable sense of man, it will be right cautiously to fit this Islamic dictum: 'God is and man is His caliph' into the poetry of Psalm viii, already cited.

> When I see the heavens, the work of your hands,
> The moon and the stars you have arranged,
> What is man, that you should keep him in mind?
> Mortal man that you care for him?
>
> You have made him little less than a god:
> With glory and honour you have crowned him,
> And gave him power over the works of your hand,
> And put all things under his feet,
> All of them, sheep and cattle,
> Yes! even the savage beasts,
> Birds of the air and fish
> That make their way through the waters.
>
> How great is your Name, O Lord our God,
> Through all the earth.[1]

In days of cybernation, the examples of human prowess may seem more than a little primitive, but the inner meaning is in no

[1] From *The Psalms: A New Translation* (Gelineau), London, 1963.

way impaired.[1] This poetic celebration of the privilege of man begins where the Qur'ān (67. 5) sets the shafts of wonder that demolish the carpings of Satan, namely, the night sky. Man, 'the weak one', is nevertheless befriended and esteemed by the celestial architect. The psalm, of course, is not properly to be quoted—as is sometimes the case—as an interrogative of paradox, but rather of acclaim: 'What is man that *you are* mindful . . .' 'With glory and with state you did crown him and made him to rule . . .' The insignificance, arguable by crudely physical criteria, is belied by the undoubted dignity, and can, indeed, be accepted with confidence, sentient as it is amid the vastnesses. The immense grandeur of the creation and the lowliness of the creature belong together, in the conviction of the psalmist. There are no wonders which do not enhance the wonder of man, since it is his greeting of their marvel by which the poetry of their meaning comes to be. What the psalm sees as the handiwork of God belongs in the cognisance of man. 'How excellent is thy Name' remains, as it were, only anonymously true, like music awaiting the musician, until the salute of human recognition gives it utterance. Yet the utterance given is ever responsive to the reality by which it is evoked. For it could never exist as a fictitious theme.

'Excellent in all the earth' the psalm declares. Praise only truly celebrates the creation when it is universal. Man the creature, through all his diversities or enmities, is one humanity, in a oneness reciprocal to the undivided sovereignty that his worship owns. In acclaiming the worth of the Name we incorporate a single humanity. That which makes vocal our adoration silences our divisions. The 'justification of life', which we saw to be the issue in Satan's conspiracy of discredit, is entire, or it is nothing— entire, that is, in the sense that God is only 'justified' when man is, that the essential truth of His praise is the integral authenticity of our being. If God, as the old saying has it, is truly 'enthroned upon the praises of His people', it is only because 'His people', one humanity, are enthroned upon His praise, responsibly entrusted,

---

[1] And verse 8 might, boldly, be claimed for the submarines, since it might read: 'He (man) passes through the tracks of the seas.'!

that is, with the business of His glory. Monotheism, in the end, is a matter of doxology, and doxology, of life. In the one praise of God we discover the one meaning and the one kinship of mankind.

It is these considerations, emerging from Psalm viii, which sustain what otherwise would have been too bold a proceeding, namely the phrasing of the theme of this Chapter: 'God is and Man is His caliph' on the pattern of the Muslim *Shahādah* itself. The reason for doing so is closely related to the meaning of the credal confession: 'There is no god but God and Muḥammad is His apostle', and if suspicion in some quarters is aroused the risk is worth taking in the hope that the connection that is in mind may dispel it.

'God is' makes, without doubt, a proper paraphrase of the first half of the Islamic witness. For the affirmation: 'There is no god but God' is clearly the negative form of a great positive, the necessary shape of a repudiation of pagan, plural, deities in the setting of Muḥammad's original mission. Disavowal of the many and confession of the One, the negative disowning and the positive proclaiming—these are inseparable and truly inter-changeable. But, going on to say: 'Man is His caliph', do we compromise the clause about the *Rasūlīyyah*, the apostolate? Hardly: if it be seen that only to caliphs can prophets be sent. It is fair to insist that only to a humanity understood in the terms we have been stating can the exhortation and the directives of messengers be relevant. In the ultimate analysis, the fact of human caliphate is simply the condition of accountability, even of addressability, which prophetic mission pre-supposes. In believing so strenuously in revelation as summoning men to obedience and conformity of will, Islam confirms the dignity that creation confers.

Is it not in the same sense that Adam is understood as the first of the messengers? His education in 'names' may be seen as part of this status, since words are the counters, not only of 'natural knowledge', but also of spiritual wisdom. Archetypal man, though solitary, is inclusive. He is the symbol of the fact that, while men are summoned by prophets to a true humanity, it is from within humanity that prophets are themselves summoned. Adam, in that sense, is both teacher and taught. He is guide and guided. He speaks as bearer the message to which he is conformable as subject. By the prophetic vocation it is the human that is mentor to the human, but only because the human in the mass is properly tributary to the prophetic in the chosen men—and both in the behalf of God.

Thus the fact of prophecy, or apostolate, as Islam receives it, assumes in a double sense the fact of the Quranic caliphate we are considering. The truth that 'only to caliphs can prophets be sent' has to be seen as including the further truth that only from caliphs can prophets come. If humanity were not constituted with this trust of the Divine will, they could neither be hearers in general nor spokesmen in particular of its claims and demands. The long history that Adam, or primal man, is seen as inaugurating is punctuated with revelatory interventions, with warnings and reminders and elucidations, aligning the human audience repeatedly with the criteria and dimensions of the human calling. That prophetic succession is seen as beginning with Adam and culminating in Muḥammad. The intent of the whole, it may be said, is the alerting of man to his privilege, its dignities, dangers and duties. Prophecy itself need not, and must not, be excluded from what that caliphate embraces. Rather, the essentially human function of the *rasūl*, or messenger—always a strong point of insistence in Quranic thought—must be acknowledged as the superlative form of man's entrustment. For that by which he is taught his trust must surely be the largest trust of all.

This must be the justification for claiming a proper affinity between the clause of the *Shahādah: Muḥammadun rasūl Allāh* and the phrase: 'Man is His caliph'. Islam has always insisted passionately on the humanity of the Prophet and his instrumentality, in wholly human terms, to the Divine purpose. We have, then, to think of the Quranic caliphate, not as something which politically takes over from Muḥammad the ruler after his death, but as that which Muḥammad consummates in his life. Or, if historical considerations require us to concede a pragmatic legitimacy to the former, it must be seen as emerging from and ancillary to the latter. For, in the end, as must be argued in Chapter V below, the Islamic justification of state sovereignty has always consisted, essentially, in the instrumentality of statehood to the Divine ends. It is those ends which are pivoted on the whole human obedience which revelation addresses and external Caliphs supposedly organized. Islamic confession, therefore, of the *rasūliyyah* of Muḥammad, proceeds necessarily within the belief in the accountable and addressable privilege of man as the term *khalīfah* enshrines it.

We return, in conclusion, to the first half of the Confession: 'God is . . .' The change from the negative: 'there is no god except God', to the positive: 'God is' presents no propositional difficulty. Either is the right form of the other, depending on the context of the witness. Confronted with idols, he is likely to need the negation first, repudiating in order to affirm. Iconoclasm achieved, the positive is all.

A propositional iconoclasm, however, is one thing: an emotional and essential one quite another. The soul that cries: 'Whom *have I* in heaven but Thee' may have so learned through crises of anguish or timidity, unknown to the abstract theologian. The crucial question, always, is not: How do we deny idols?—often an easy enough proceeding—but how do we dethrone them in the hearts of their worshippers? In this sense the Decalogue, with its 'Thou shalt *have* none other gods but Me,' concerns itself with the imperative of unity rather than with the bare affirmative. It is precisely this 'existential' disqualifying of the false deities, as distinct from their simple disavowal, that the caliphate of man makes possible.

For the falsity and tyranny of the pseudo-gods have to be broken in two directions. It is not only that they usurp the sovereignty properly God's alone, but also that they deprive and deprave mankind and by their intimidation preclude the true authority and liberty of man's 'imperium'. A polytheistic society is necessarily a prey to fears, insecurities, phobias and vagaries, as it peoples the diverse phenomena of the world with demonic forces, or *baalīm*, and subjugates itself, by these beliefs, to all manner of propitiatory devices and protective rites. The one path of liberation is in the realization of the psalmist: 'The Lord is my shepherd, I will fear no evil.' The single and relevant Divine mastery obviates and expels all plural powers and tyrannies. But the other path, reciprocal to the first, is the active discovery of the human competence, the understanding that the 'have thou dominion' of Genesis and the caliphate of the Qur'ān are an implicit emancipation from all nature-based idolatries and the apprehensions of pluralizing superstition.

It is sometimes supposed that 'science' is the bestower of these liberties. It would be truer to see it as the acceptance of them. Certainly the actual nullification of the fears that go with polytheism owes very much to scientific development. But the latter, however slow and fitful its history, is only rightly seen as the appropriation of the elemental, original endowment of man. The cumulative, and now awesome, empire of men in technology achieves in unprecedented degree the ancient prerogatives of mankind, as Biblical and Quranic faith receives them. Far from being wrung, defiantly, from an oppressive or grudging heaven, they are no more, however changed in degree, than the essential, unchanging charter of human vicegerency.

It is this which effectively dethrones and dismisses the pseudo-deities. We may call it if we will 'desacralization', if, thereby, we mean an ousting of the *baals*, the idols, the fickle powers, believed to harry, threaten or tantalize mankind from within the processes of the natural order. But it is a tragic error to equate that proper human authority in the routing of the gods many and lords many, with the single lordship to which that authority returns and by whose ungrudging sovereignty it enjoys its mighty privilege. We have heard too much in recent years of religious faith as, allegedly, an incubus on investigative study and of the sense of the Divine as thwarting a truly human liberty in the midst of things. The truth, on the contrary, is that the human competence and the Divine dimension belong in one. It takes omnipotence to bestow what man enjoys: it takes submission to receive it worthily.

Where polytheism enslaves or tyrannizes, science emancipates. But the appeal to unity by which it does so forbids new profanations or idolatries of its own pretension.

It is for this reason that 'secularization' is so potentially misleading a name for the technological masteries we now possess. They have certainly ended the divinization of nature, but in so doing have in no way impaired the sacred. They have simply terminated the ignorance and superstition that gave the sacred a falsely plural and chaotic form. The hallowedness of the natural abides, not less but more imperative in the new intensity of its human entrustment, the new urgency of its human fate.

What is now a quite daunting amenability of the world to man's manipulation and exploitation surely makes correspondingly more crucial the acknowledgement and acceptance of its sanctity. Science has changed the themes of idolatry but in no way eliminated its dangers. Technology, truly, banishes the deities of a sacral superstition, but gives excuse for seductive pretensions of its own. Is the menace of a demonic history necessarily preferable to the vagaries of a nature populated with gods? The science that ends the idols of simple fear begets the idols of pride in the autocracies the same science creates. It tempts us to make absolute the goals for which it yields unlimited means and in a desacralized nature we bow down the more readily to power, or race or nation, to sex or greed or gain, or we divinize ourselves in sloth, or waste, or boredom.

The answer is not, of course, some archaic return to the prescientific reverence by which men stood in sacred awe within the world but, instead, to renew the sacredness of the 'imperium' itself, to know it there from the beginning however lowly its achievement, and confess that the liberties we call the 'secular' are no more than new dimensions of the age-long and hallowed prerogative of man. Experiencing, as we do in our generation, in unprecedented fullness, the reality of our human dominion, the more insistently are we summoned to confess it as a gift and to hold it in radical reverence, subduing and refusing the idolatries to which it is prone. To affirm, in a world like ours, with its massive tokens of the competence and the bedevilment of man, that 'there is no god but God', is squarely to deny the final sovereignty to the human yet also splendidly to proclaim a Divine lordship of the utmost magnanimity and grace. To confess that man is caliph is to acknowledge a dignity now known to be so generous as to argue a bestowing goodness so secure as to risk so large a liberty and set servants in so large a room. This conclusion is sufficient reason for setting firmly within the central creed of Islam this other assurance that man is 'His caliph'.

The Divine lordship, then, is real in addressing a truly emancipated recognition of it. Only in the human caliphate are the false gods disqualified, whether as the tyrannies born of fears our competence dispels, or as pseudo-absolutes our true submission breaks. It is in the viceroy, rightly reigning and truly serving, that the 'gods' are disowned. Or, in the Qur'ān's most insistent terminology, *Shirk* ends when there are no longer *mushrikūn*. 'There is no god but God' becomes true, in its truth, when men 'have none other gods but Him'. Man's undivided worship is the mirror of the Divine unity, and in that sense his caliphate is the condition God has willed for His glory in creation.

Are we not close here to the ultimate meaning of 'the jealous God'? Not a phrase which the Qur'ān uses, it is none the less akin to the whole concern of the Muslim Scripture for an undiverted worship and its steady indictment of idolatry as 'great wrong'. For 'the jealous God'—or may we perhaps more rightly say, 'the zealous God'?—is not, as so often sadly supposed, the God whose rule is oppressively suspicious of human action and sternly inimical to human joys and powers. Such a notion is utterly excluded by the truths we have considered. We may totally repudiate any such Divine antipathy to man. It is the true stature of the intended viceroy that both inspires and demands the 'zeal of the Lord'. It is the stake of the Divine in the human, the fulfilment of the human in the Divine, that arouses 'the jealousy' of God. Satan, calumniously, urges that man is a worthless risk. God is well enough aware of the same crisis, but with the patient carefulness of expectancy.

III

'His Secretarie, Abraham'

The world was created for the sake of Abraham. As for this great mass (the earth), for what end is it here? For the sake of Abraham, as it is said: 'Thou hast made the heaven and the earth, and Thou didst choose Abraham.' (Neh. ix. 6–7).

So, reportedly, the Rabbis Joshua b Karḥa and Azariah.[1] The Biblical history seems to confirm it, in moving so rapidly from the primeval to the patriarchal, from the theme of creation to the story of the great prototype of the righteous man, the 'friend of God'. There is a paradox, to which we will attend in the next Chapter, inherent in a figure who is at once the index to the human privilege and the founder of a unique people. For the moment, however, we simply take the words as meaning that the world is meant for man as man is meant in Abraham. It was for the sake of a humanity in Abrahamic terms that the created order came to be. The sacred history opens on the stage of nature with a personal drama to embody and exemplify the proper manner of mankind.

In this sense of their verdict, the Rabbis are of course sustained by the whole consensus of Semitic faiths. Judaism, Christianity and Islam alike concur in esteeming Abraham as the first of the faithful, the father of the people of God, the true ḥanīf or God-fearer, the pilgrim seeker of the city of God among men. There are, as we must trace, significant differences of emphasis in the role of Abraham among the three systems. But there is no doubt of his definitive status as the single founder and exemplar of their communities—the man of faith in true possession of existence,

[1] Quoted from Bereshit, xii, 9, in C. G. Montefiore and H. Loewe, *A Rabbinic Anthology*, London, 1938, p. 38.

the due representative of God, the custodian who truly bears and
hallows the divine Name.

It fits well, therefore, to borrow from Hakluyt's *Voyages*,
quoting the familiar Muslim tradition about Abraham and
Ishmael and the Ka'bah at Mecca, the happy archaism that
suggests our title phrase: 'The mercifull God commanded his
secretarie Abraham to build him a house in Mecca.'[1] For the
secretarius is the one who has the secret in good keeping, whose
mind is privy to his master's purpose and committed to its
service. 'The secret of the Lord', says the psalmist, 'is with them
that fear Him and He will show them his covenant.' The word,
all the better for its quaintness in this sense, puts us in the way of
the privilege of man as understood of Abraham among our faiths.
The hope in what follows is to carry forward the theme emerging
from the Quranic 'caliphate' and the Biblical 'dominion' of
Adam, or man, by pondering in the same sources and their sequel
this prince of patriarchal figures. May we take in George Herbert
on the way? He writes:

> Of all the creatures both in sea and land,
> Only to man Thou hast made known thy ways,
> And put the pen alone into his hand
> And made him secretary of thy praise . . .
> Man is the world's high priest: he doth present
> The sacrifice for all: while they below
> Unto the sacred service mutter an assent,
> Such as springs use that fall, or winds that blow.[2]

Islam shrinks from such priestly metaphors, but sees man according to the Qur'ān as 'taught the use of the pen'—as noted in the
previous Chapter—in order to indite the praises of God. Scribe to
the universe is a human title in no way averse to the temper of the
Qur'ān, with its perception of the Divine glory and its eminent
status as revelation and literature in one. Rabbinic traditions, also,
link Abraham with such a role in the education of thanksgiving:

---

[1] *Voyages*, II. i. 209. The Oxford Dictionary observes *in loco* that Chaucer's
'Wife of Bath was too full of chinks to be a good secretarie'.

[2] *Providence*.

'Abraham used to entertain the passers by. When they had eaten and drunk he said to them: "Speak the blessing." They said: "What are we to say?" He replied: "Say, Blessed be the Lord of the world, of whose gifts we have eaten."'[1]

A necessary prelude, however, to any study of man in Abraham, or of Abraham as the authentic measure of the human calling, is the question of historicity. How are we to take so remote a figure, mediated in scriptural terms through so many sequences of oral tradition? How does the present documentary shape of his story reflect the actual circumstances of a personal emigration and a spiritual odyssey? How far ought it to be taken as a focus of plural movements of tribal migration, idealized into patriarchal legend? Can primary strands of the tradition be isolated so as to determine the precise motives of the expedition from Ur, and the journey into Canaan? What are the sure elements in the theophanies and what is their relation to local centres, Hebron in particular? How is the fragment that forms Genesis xiv, the narrative of the pursuit and defeat of the five kings, to be explained and assessed within the general picture and what is the real significance of that puzzling figure Melchizedek and his blessing of Abraham? On the Quranic side there are the further questions about Abraham in the Hijāz and the attribution to him of the building of the Ka'bah in Mecca.[2] There is ample room for conjecture and academic ingenuity in the minutiae of these issues as far as archaeology, research and textual study can elucidate them.[3]

For present purposes, however, there is neither place nor occasion for these complexities. Our concerns in the human caliphate in its Abrahamic measure do not, of course, dismiss historicity, but they certainly transcend it. In the last resort it is

[1] Montefiore and Loewe, op. cit., p. 282.

[2] Ṭāhā Ḥusain, in Al-Sha'ir al-Jāhilī, Cairo, 1926 (re-issued with some changes in 1927 as Al-Adab al-Jāhilī), provides a well-known example of the sensitivities attaching to this theme.

[3] As, for example, M. C. Astour's 'Political and Cosmic Symbolism in Genesis 14 and its Babylonian Sources', in Biblical Motifs: Origins and Transformations, edited by Alexander Altmann, Cambridge, Mass., 1966, pp. 65–109.

not facticity about Abraham that matters, even if it were indubit–
ably recoverable. The important thing is what Abraham was
believed to have been and how tradition possessed him. The facts
of belief, here, embodying the shape of his authority over thought
and behaviour, are in their way more solid and relevant than those
that a 'pure' history might try, at best very approximately, to
regain as the facts of events. What, for example, is the 'pure'
historian to make of Mount Moriah and the binding of Isaac?
The ultimate responsibility of history here is to the dimensions
the Abrahamic 'legend' gave to Hebrew religion and to Islamic
faith, seeing those dimensions as the form, in corporate memory
and apprehension, of the deep transactions of a history able to
beget them. In this sense Abraham is what Abraham's 'family'
say he is. The Abraham of veneration and obedience is the
Abraham of historical importance, unless we are to subordinate
the 'event' of formative interpretation through the centuries to
the event of the 'original' past in its remote particulars. The former
'happened' no less concretely than the latter and did so much
more consequentially. This is not, of course, to imply that scholarship has no business with the exploration of the story of Abraham,
its sources and evidences. It is simply to insist that the exemplari-
ness of Abraham, as father of nations, as ḥanīf and iconoclast, as
'friend of God', is the ultimate historical factor, rather than elusive
material of place and time and sequence out of which it came.
What matters is *millat Ibrahīm*, as the Qur'ān puts it, the community or posterity of this devotion and their sense of this descent
from the great begetter of their spirits. Abraham believed is
Abraham.

Pursuing that confidence without neglect of history, we discover in Abraham what may be identified, in broad general
terms, as the three constitutive emphases of the three faiths. As
founder figure, he comprises the aspects which predominate in
the great systems which derive from him and which might be
described very widely as the ethnic, the pragmatic and the
sacrificial. It is imperative to say at once that these elements, which
must be carefully studied and substantiated, are in no sense rigidly

to be confined to the community they most readily characterize. On the contrary, there is a quite striking inter-penetration, as we shall see, whereby Jewry, Islam and Christianity participate deeply in what they hold to be definitive of each other. Yet 'seed', 'standing' and 'suffering'—in the Abrahamic shape of each— seem properly to be taken as, in a primary way, the clue to the Hebraic, the Muslim and the Christian heritage in Abraham. The aim of this Chapter is to consider this threefold significance of the patriarchal image as a prelude, strangely anticipatory in its content, to the pattern of the human privilege as received in each faith.

'SEED': ABRAHAM OUR FATHER

There can be little doubt that this is the primary Biblical emphasis. The Old Testament is aware of the pioneer figure as, first and foremost, the progenitor of a people. 'In thee and in thy seed shall all the nations of the earth bless themselves.' The focus of the Genesis narrative on the Isaac awaited, received, jeopardized and restored, and the 'aberration' of Ishmael's advent as the result of miscalculating impatience, alike point up the central motif of the crucial, and the proper, progeny, ensuring the perpetuation of the true seed. As a study in the pain and dismay of childlessness it might be loosely paralleled in any human story, Semitic, African, or where-ever one wills, only that here is the mystery of destiny sharpening the ordinary distress of the barren womb. Sarah has no 'little laughter', no laughter at all, and greets with ironical and incredulous laughter the mysterious rekindling of the promise that weary, empty years had seemed to extinguish. The word of Abraham's expectancy appeared as sterile as Sarah's womb. Hope deferred, and finally almost extinct, gives way to a sudden, late, in-credible reprieve. Isaac is born 'according to the promise', doubly so, in the sense of the Divine pledge originally given and the re-demption of the pledge in the last, impossible extremity of years.

The seed and the promise, as the history sees them, are together contrasted with the episode of Hagar and the half-son, the child of disquieted action in neglect of the promise—a neglect of which Abraham is guilty by inferring the negligence of God. We have no means of knowing what obscure traditions of tribal movements and enmities lie behind these narratives—though we know tragically well the tensions and postures of hostility they have projected into later history. But the immediate interest of the Genesis documents is to emphasize the right succession, endangered as it had been, first by delay, then by distraction, and finally redeemed by a near miracle of fulfilment. This, it may be said, is a narrative form of the over-riding sense of particular election. The patriarchal crisis, as it were, reflects the abiding preciousness of the chosen people, their continuity always crucial and retrieved from all odds by the Divine favour. The seed, we may say, achieved in Isaac, and contrasted by Hagar, is set forth by the tradition in Genesis, as inalienable, providential, precarious, singular and unique. Election bides its time, keeps its counsel and makes good its ends. These are lessons that persist through the whole sequence of the history.

The Abrahamic seed, however, begins in an exile's courage, the founding of a people in a family migration. Whereas, as we shall see, the Quranic emphasis in this initial *Hijrah*, or venture, of Abraham, is the vehement repudiation of idols, the Genesis narrative concentrates firmly on the inauguration of a family history in a new territory. Both the Genesis accounts in Chaps. xi and xii, and other summaries elsewhere in the Old Testament, make no mention of iconoclasm, though Joshua xxiv. 2 confirms that Terah, Abraham's father, and his people 'served other gods'. It seems right, therefore, to conclude that the Old Testament means Abraham's travels to be taken as the setting, if not the cause, the crux rather than the sequel, of his 'conversion'. It would appear that he found liberation from idols by journeying itself, in the care and company of the family deity, whereas the Quranic Abraham is an idol-breaker within his family and city. The Biblical picture concentrates on the interior experience, the private summons, leading to the awareness of a relationship expressed in the phrase, 'the God of Abraham'.

Genesis records the migration from Ur of the Chaldees to Canaan in two stages, the first apparently initiated by Terah, and the second, after a prolonged interval, by Abraham. Haran, where Terah died, marks the place of the intervening sojourn. It is probable that there is also a sort of half-way house out of a plural worship. Haran may be regarded as still familiar territory of the moon-god worshipped, as a cultic deity, by Terah in Ur. Leonard Woolley has argued strongly for the steady waning of the moon-god in Ur in the generations immediately preceding Abraham, with a consequent deepening of devotion to the minor gods of family protection and veneration.[1] His view is based on impressive evidence of the growing cult of the family dead and the domestic shrines.

The full implication of this in the case of Abraham did not become apparent until, by departure from Haran, he passed finally out from under the aegis of the moon-god and was cast in an exclusive sort of way upon the power of the family deity. The exclusive then became, by the sheer fact of travel, an inclusifying experience of that same deity in the vicissitudes of new circumstances and territories. It seems a fair conjecture to suppose that a sort of extra-territoriality of 'the God of Abraham' developed in Abraham's mind. He travelled with a sense of a personal Divine aegis. As a clan or family 'patron' 'the God of Abraham' was in no way identifiable with the natural phenomena Abraham encountered as he journeyed—phenomena which, whether in their benison or their menace, would be readily linked with nature deities of other territories, interchangeable as these phenomena are. As the deity of a single, sufficient confidence on Abraham's part, 'the God of Abraham' remained securely distinct from any local or clan gods in the new lands that Abraham penetrated. And not only distinct: for by virtue of Abraham's trust, He took over the cares and powers which any different, superstitious traveller would have conceded instinctively to the local cults. But precisely by taking over these protective and sponsoring functions for His servant, Abraham's God was seen, in that experience, to have the competence and the writ of power which territorial pluralism of worships never understood. In this way it was the very exile of Abraham, his adventure of

[1] Leonard Woolley, *Abraham*, London, 1935.

faith, which made his emancipation. The crucial principle of a sufficient reliance and the fact of an expatriate together shaped the sense of a Divine relationship, at once sure, ubiquitous and adequate. It was a discovery which no keepers-at-home would ever have made, about a lordship which none of their clan cults could have wrested from the cosmic or the nature gods.

If this reading of the story has rightly conjectured what lies within that vital phrase 'the God of Abraham', then there is clearly a deep reciprocity between the Divine reality and Abraham's faith. That fact alone is enough to suggest the conclusion is right. For reciprocity of the worshipped and the worshipper, the trusted and trusting, is constantly characteristic of Hebraic religion. God is, in this sense, what faith and thanksgiving take Him to be. With Abraham, no less than with Moses at the bush and in the Exodus, it is the event which 'makes Him known'. Being expatriate is the condition within which the man of active faith experiences the faithworthiness of the power within the calling that he believes to have initiated his ventures. 'The Lord had said unto Abram: Get thee out of thy country . . . and from thy father's house.' (Gen. xii. 1.) By his very journeying into strange lands, Abraham stakes the claim of a deity who, aside from such a discipleship, would have been excluded as an interloper. Abraham refused to exchange that original reliance, born of family origins, for the protectors that new localities would otherwise have imposed. For he was neither a timid fugitive embracing whatever he found, nor yet a craven soul staying where familiar securities were bounded. He and His Lord were on the road together. Expatriation and assurance were two sides of one experience.

Until the call of Moses (Exodus iii and vi) this God has no name, other than that which links Him with His 'friend'—though the usage 'of Abraham' is by its very meaning capable of recurrence in the forms 'of Isaac' and 'of Jacob', and that, not merely in the sense that these are 'in the loins of Abraham', but that the same pattern can be reproduced in their own biographies, however contrasted their characters. 'The God of Abraham' is also, historically 'the God of Nahor, the God of their father', as Laban's oath-proposal to Jacob declares in Gen. xxi. 53. Yet He is, in the new predicates of Abraham's existence, a strikingly different deity. For the meaning of that family custodian in Ur has been radically enlarged and transformed by the education Abraham's biography had given him. The identity is echoed again in Gen. xv. 7, 'I am the Lord who brought thee out of Ur', where the words, as Woolley observes, refer to the time when Abraham had merely gone along with Terah.[1] It was the Abrahamic ventures out of Haran that gave genesis, out of that pluralism, to the unitary theology of Old Testament experience. The discovery of the Divine reality marches, we may surely say, with the exemplification of the privilege of man. God and Abraham, so to speak, enter history together: for history, Biblically, is the meaning of their friendship.

What, in the immediate context of this exposition, is to be said about Genesis xxii, the call to offer Isaac, and the deep pathos of his 'binding' in the traditions of Jewry? It is intended to reserve the theme of Moriah and the lamb for the Christian possession of Abraham, in the third phase of this Chapter, not in any sense to isolate their New Testament bearing from their immense Jewish significance but only in order to gain the advantage of seeing these together. Meanwhile, may we not recognize, in the Genesis xxii narrative, a great crisis in this same Abrahamic discovery of the sovereignty of 'his' God over all causes, and that in the most compelling form? It would seem that there can be little doubt that the testing of Abraham, in the terms of this event, means a profound repudiation of human sacrifice. The substitution of the ram caught in a thicket, for the son, asserts in the whole sacrificial realm the uniqueness of the human, and by a decisive exemption holds it inalienably to and for that Divine relationship of living community which Abraham enjoys and which, apart from this unmistakeable veto, might have been held susceptible of the same travesties of the human truth exacted by heathen practices.

Isaac is, thus, not only the proper son, awaited according to

[1] *Ibid.*, pp. 237–8.

promise, but also the inviolate son, retrieved, by decisive reckoning, from the precarious fate of a pagan progeny always in
jeopardy from the demands of the gods. The God of Abraham
eloquently restores to His servant's keeping the only son of his
chosen line. All the subsequent implications of the 'binding' of
Isaac belong with developments in the history of the people which
were entirely unknown in the context of Abraham's journey to
the mount. Nor does the passage conjecture any interpretation
hingeing on anticipation of a 'passion' of Israel at the hands of
enemy nations. This fact is the more remarkable if we are to
suppose, as some scholars do, that the narrative of Genesis xxii
reflects experiences of later history. Isaac may well become a
symbol of life out of death and hope out of tragedy, capable of
application, as Christian usage showed, to situations of calamity
and despair. But in its own context the story has to do solely with
the inner actions of Abraham himself and these in no way stand
for external menace or circumstantial peril. If, by a forced exegesis,
we compel them to do so we forfeit the whole interior dimension
of Abraham's obedience. He is reacting, not to a mortal danger
he cannot elude but to an inward impulse he cannot ignore. To
take his son alive again from off the faggots and from under the
knife of his own fatherly oblation is to know indubitably the son
that he is. The 'seed' of Abraham becomes a hallowed re-
assurance through a deliberate transaction. Forfeiture is willed
and possession becomes unbroken: each are a measure of 'friendship' with God.

The 'mountain' of the ascent of Abraham and Isaac, described
in the story as 'one of the mountains' of 'the land of Moriah',
has a traditional identity with the rock of the Temple area in
Jerusalem. As a tradition it links us with Melchizedek, King of
Salem, the mysterious figure who, in the Genesis xiv narrative,
greeted Abraham on returning from the defeat of the five kings.
We need not hope to unravel all the perplexities attaching to this
passage to recognize its central implication as an act of tribute to
Abraham's spirited exercise of will in the defence of family
interests. The adventure implicit in his voluntary exile from

Haran has its counterpart in his successful assertion of the physical patrimony within the new territory. 'Seed' and land are always in close relationship in the Old Testament view, and the bond between them makes for the third element, the political. The continuity of the generations pre-supposes a sustained occupancy, an assured homeland, as its ground and pledge. These in turn demand the sinews of force, and prowess, for their securing. Abraham is seen in Genesis xiv as an able practitioner of this art and the priest-king of Salem sets a kind of sacramental seal upon his activity.

It has been noted that the circular itinerary of the five kings in the conquests which Abraham's small band of retainers undoes follows, in reverse direction, the route taken, according to Deuteronomy i to iii, by the tribes after the Exodus and the wilderness sojourn.[1] May there be a deliberate association here with the campaigns of Joshua and an interest on the part of the historians in asserting, by this precedent, both the wide reach of Abraham's heritage and the proper authority of Jerusalemite priesthood? Be the answer as it may, there is no mistaking the broad significance of the Abrahamic as including this necessary dimension of vigorous action in the preservation of the home of the 'seed'. Yet, present as this element is in the fascinating, if also puzzling, shape of this narrative, the primary emphasis is not political but ethnic, not activist but faithful. Abraham dominates the early history in Genesis, not as the resourceful conqueror of Chedorlaomer, but as the emigrant from Haran, the father of a people, the patriarch whose supreme crises had to do with being childless, first by long deferment of hope and then by fearful apprehension. In that experience, possessed and perpetuated by collective memory, we have the meaning of human birth and the Hebraic measure of man. The 'seed' is the privilege.

THE *Islām* OF ABRAHAM

The Qur'ān differs remarkably from Genesis in the general picture of the great progenitor of faith. There are, of course, essential

---

[1] See M. C. Astour, *loc. cit.*, p. 108.

elements in common but there is no mistaking the contrasts. With its characteristic distrust of 'chosen people', the Muslim Scripture discounts the theme of hereditary community and, therefore, of Abraham as founder of such a status. Instead it centres its interest on a courageous iconoclasm and sees Abraham as anticipating in his Sumerian abode the qualities and patterns of Muḥammad at Mecca. The distinction is almost explicit in Surah 2. 124: '"Behold, I make you a leader for the people." Said he: "And of my seed?" He (God) said: "My covenant shall not reach the evildoers."' Exegesis has built a considerable political science upon this verse in relation to its disqualification of the hereditary principle. However that may be, it does seem plainly to dissociate the stature of Abraham himself from any necessary continuity in his family. It is not, of course, possible for the Qur'ān to detach itself from the deep Biblical concern with the succession of generations. But it is always sharply insistent on the necessity of personal fidelity and castigates any reliance on the mere notion of posterity to Abraham. It is in this context that we must set its exchange of Isaac for Ishmael in the central position and its association of Ishmael with Abraham in the actual enterprise of erecting the Ka'bah in Mecca as the focus of a pure worship.

There are, no doubt, aspects of Arab independence of non-Arab elements in this emphasis on Ishmael, some of which will appear in the discussion in Chapter V. Islam is not without a certain 'ethnic' quality, with its Arabic Qur'ān and its Arab Prophet. But these factors, inseparable as they are from historical genesis of faith and community, in no way equal in degree, or rival in intention, the Hebraic sense of God's choice of a people. Indeed, the Quranic philosophy of history, its sense of moral impartialities of requital, its faith in revelation via a scripture, all combine to displace Old Testament election from the centre of the stage and to constitute prophetic vigour the primary vehicle of the Divine will.

Here the robust Quranic Abraham comes into his own. Whereas Genesis records Abraham's summons to emigrate in obedience to a destiny in a new land and gives no hint of a crusading temper in the old, the Qur'ān in several passages sets him at the centre of a strenuous denunciation of idolatry. Thus Surah 37. 81–97.

Of his (Noah's) party was also Abraham:
When he came to his Lord with a perfect heart,
When he said to his father and his people:
'What do you serve?
A lie! Gods other than God do you desire?
What think you then of the Lord of all being?'
Then he turned a glance to the stars
And said: 'It sickens me.'
But, turning their backs on him, they went off.
Then, addressing their gods, he said:
'What do you eat? What ails you that you do not speak?'
He turned on them and struck them with his right hand.
Then came the others to him with haste.
'Do you serve what you hew?' he asked them,
'When God created both you and what you manufacture!'

His family and townsfolk conspired to destroy him. There are the same elements in other passages—courage, a sense of indignation born of the contemplation of nature's mystery, a powerful irony and vehement controversy with his own people. All these make, in the language of Surah 21. 51, the *rushd* of Abraham—his true guidance and his right course. The passage, with echoes of an old talmudic story, goes on to describe the gist of the argument. Like all traditionalists, Abraham's folk protest that their worship of gods is inherited from their forebears. They question whether Abraham is not trifling with their fears. He replies with the claim that he speaks for the Creator, the Lord of the worlds, and assures them he will disprove the idols. He shatters all but the largest of them and when his people return, vowing vengeance on the perpetrator of this enormity, the 'young man', Abraham, being identified as the guilty iconoclast, chides them with the story that the big idol had battered all the rest. Incredulous, they take him for the culprit and threaten him with death by fire. Undaunted,

Abraham mocks their barren trust in idols who cannot secure themselves from human blows and God cools the fire of his persecutors.[1]

In a further passage, in Surah 29. 15 f., Abraham enlarges the appeal to nature with familiar Quranic invocation to gratitude and to a sense of the evident visitations of human history. Surah 26 returns to the same themes, reproves slavish persistence in the ancestral errors, and records Abraham's prayer for his father, 'for he is one of those astray' (26. 86). The tension of family loyalty and prophetic truth is nowhere more poignant than in Surah 19. 41-9.

And in the Book make mention of Abraham, true man and prophet. He said thus to his father: 'Father, why do you serve what neither hears, nor sees, what avails you nothing? Father, I have come to know what you have not: so come my way and I will guide you in a level path. Father, do not worship Satan; Satan is rebellious against the All merciful. Father, I fear the nemesis on you of the All merciful, you being tributary to Satan.' He replied: 'O Abraham, are you abandoning my gods? Give o'er, else I will surely stone you. Hence, away.' 'Peace be upon you,' he said. 'I will ask forgiveness for you from my Lord. He is good to me. I will not keep company with you or with your idols. I will call upon my Lord alone and cast myself upon His answer not adverse!'

Reflection makes it clear that Muḥammad's own conflict in Mecca is mirrored in these precedents, and that the whole impulse to the exodus of the patriarch from his patrimony is not so much a prospective inheritance as a present repudiation. These aspects, it may be said, need not be excluded from the Old Testament picture: they are certainly congruent with the intention of Hebrew history. But they are not there explicit. It is not so much travel, in itself, which, Quranically, accomplishes the 'conversion' of Abraham, but rather the contemplation of the heavens, the

---

[1] Is there perhaps a discernible, if unintended, meaning here in the one big god left after devouring all the little ones? Certainly big absolutes in history have a way of absorbing smaller ones and small lies are overtaken by bigger ones.

consideration of the stars.[1] Surah 6. 74 f. makes this plain. Abraham in these verses learns to perceive that there is no Divine title in the planets. The stars, the moon and the sun, alike, set and give way to the dark. While Abraham's people fear to withhold worship from these powers of the heavens, he fears rather lest he confound them with the Divine majesty creating and sustaining them. *Allāhu akbar*: 'greater is God'. This *ḥujjah*, or 'case', of Abraham against the associators provides a rallying ground, a nucleus for the truly faithful, and thus leads to the crucial Quranic concept of *Millat Ibrāhīm*—the party, or community, of Abraham.

The term *millah* has passed into Islamic history as denoting any corporate 'collective' cohering around religious persuasion. In the original, Abrahamic, sense, however, it defines this shared conviction of a true worship in its necessary militancy against the fashion of idolatry. The ancestral paganism, against which Abraham, and likewise Muḥammad, rebelled, was already sanctioned by community adherence. Indeed, as we have seen, this persistence—shall we call it tyranny?—of the generations past was the formidable aspect of the prophets' task. The solidarity of misguided beliefs, extending through the sequence of generations, could only be broken by the genesis of a new, 'confessional' solidarity grounded in the prophetic message and its community of response. Taking Abraham as the first prototype of such a rallying spirit, the Qur'ān sees the *Millah* of Abraham as, therefore, the great synonym for incorporate Islam. It comes almost to mean a 'nation', consisting, however, in the firm, and total, 'party-ship' of the right worship and the true obedience. As such, it contrasts with, and stands over against, the historic identities of Jewry and Christendom. Thus Surah 2. 135, for example, distinguishes Abraham's 'folk' from both these precedent communities, while Surah 22. 78 links the term 'muslims' with Abraham's usage as a descriptive of his *Millah*.[2]

The Quranic dissociation of Abraham from the two communities

---

[1] Our English 'consideration' derives, of course, from the stars (Latin: *sidus, sideris*, a constellation) as being, no doubt, the first direction of man's attentiveness.

[2] Other passages are 2. 130; 3. 95; 4. 125; 6. 161; 12. 38; 16. 123.

traditionally owning his ancestry, prior to Islam, is a clear measure of the vigour and assurance of the Islamic attachment to the founder figure. The will to exclusify that relationship, to claim it uniquely for Islam, has to be taken as indicating its insistent divergence from both Jewish and Christian reception of his significance. The Islamic dimensions read in Abraham are not additional, but alternative, themes, and involve a disavowal of received history in the name of what is claimed as a truer image. Abraham has, so to speak, to be de-ethnicized, over against Jewry, before he can be authentically known. This is part of the implication in the intriguing term, *hanif*, frequently applied to the patriarch in close connection with the *millah* usage. Whatever its import in the Meccan setting of Muhammad himself, it is applied to Abraham in this sense of 'neither Jew nor Christian'. Its positive meaning seems to point to some form of godfearingness, or concern for unitary worship and moral rectitude, such as Abraham exemplified in his crusade against the idols of his people. In both senses it fits with the independence and the concern of original Islam.

By the sturdy activism implicit in these aspects of the *muslim* Abraham, we can more readily appreciate the simple dimension of the political which belongs with him in the Qur'ān. It emerges, not as in Genesis xiv, in respect of a vigorous counter-action against marauding forces, but rather in the form of 'establishment' and its loyal security. Surah 2. 258, in a passage that is not immediately clear, refers to the 'kingdom' given to Abraham by his Lord. The context involves a disputant who questions the Divine power and Abraham's replies cite the mysteries of life and death and of the sunrise. Whether these are to be taken as signs, or precedents, for the rise of Abraham as a leader in history is not certain. There is even a question among commentators as to whether the 'kingdom' is not grammatically assignable to Abraham's opponent, as a token in support of his disbelief, i.e. a successful idolater presuming on his prestige. However, in Surah 4. 54 there is reference to 'a mighty Kingdom' given to the people of Abraham, together with the Book and the Wisdom. Here again, though, the verse throws no unequivocal light on the external form of Abraham's personal hegemony in Mecca. All we can say is that there is a general association in the Qur'ān between the fact of an Abrahamic centre in the city and a concern on its founder's part for its perpetuation in peace and prosperity.

Necessarily, in this context, the sense of the 'seed' recurs, but there is a marked difference of temper compared with the Old Testament. The prayer for the securing of Mecca (Surah 2. 120 f. and 14. 35 f.) is linked explicitly with prayer for a godly, submissive lineal succession: 'Turn me and my sons away from idol-serving.' And 'Whoever follows me belongs to me'. Blood-worth is conditional upon faith, and faith constitutes incorporation. The words that follow in 14. 36: 'Whoever rebels against me (Abraham), surely Thou art All forgiving' might be taken to suggest a sort of 'political' element ('aṣānī may have that implication), but the concluding clause lifts the issue to a very different level. Abraham's 'establishment' in the city of Muḥammad's birth is, by these Quranic criteria, not a tribal state claiming some implicit Divine sanction or safeguard, but rather a sanctuary entrusted to a custody turning on fidelity, with the generations making, or unmaking, their own loyalty. Abraham seeks only a right continuity and bespeaks for this the Divine benison of a natural prosperity. 'Praise be to God, who has given me, old as I am, Ishmael and Isaac: surely my Lord is the hearer of prayer' (14. 39).

This, then, in its Quranic initiation, is 'the station of Abraham'. If it is to be seen as a state, it is modest in the extreme, with no guaranteed line—since faith is critical in each generation—and no pledged perpetuation in line of descent or political order. Its only legacy to future legists or partisans is the fundamental idea of a focal point of religious loyalties, in a living protection of the faithful, and open to the access, both physical and spiritual of all who will, as a place at once of immunity and peace. (See Surah 3. 97.) Abraham's odyssey, it might be said, had repudiated tribe and state in the name of worship. His settlement stakes in a right worship the pride of tribe and state. The first great iconoclast is not a founder of Caliphates: he contents himself with the caliphate of prayer. He is the architect, not of a dynasty, but of a sanctuary.

ABRAHAM: THE THIRD DIMENSION

Jewry's founder-father and Islam's founder idol-breaker and inaugurator of the holy city has, in the Biblical record in both Testaments, a third secret. Its focus is the narrative of Genesis xxii, set, of course, in the whole context that gives it meaning. The Qur'ān refers only briefly to the 'sacrifice' of Isaac (Surah 37. 97–111) which it places in the context of a dream. Isaac is only mentioned by name in the sequel to the story. The willing son is ransomed after Abraham had stood the test and earned the benediction of posterity: 'Peace be upon Abraham.' For Hebrew tradition, in retrospect, the whole story is seen as a portent of tragedy and immolation. For persecuted Jewry, Isaac becomes a ready symbol of a people thrust into supreme jeopardy and living in the perpetual necessity of proving its fidelity in the very sacrifice of its life.

Inwardly authentic as this belief is in the Isaac quality of Hebrew experience among the nations, it turns, nevertheless, upon the parallel sense of chosenness and the 'seed'. The core of the Christian reception of the third dimension of Abraham consists in its discovery of this mystery of sacrifice and peril in transcendence of the particularity which gives it Jewish point. What 'is seen in the mount of the Lord', to quote the play on words in Gen. xxii. 14, is taken and perceived in the New Testament as a universal truth of losing to find and dying to live. Having learned, in the immediate terms of the Genesis historian, the inviolability of the 'seed', and the sanctity of man, we discern, through Christ, the larger, inclusive, mystery of grace and its lengths.

Perhaps the best way in to this hallowed ground is to ponder the Abrahamic situations in which there are no substitutes for Isaac because the crisis of his 'binding' arises from impulses that heed no restraining word and are bent only on destruction.

Wilfred Owen caught them grimly in his poem: *The Parable of the Old Man and the Young:*

> Then Abram bound the youth with belts and straps,
> And builded parapets and trenches there,
> And stretched forth the knife to slay his son,
> When, lo! an angel called him out of heaven,
> Saying, lay not thine hand upon the lad,
> Neither do anything to him. Behold,
> A ram caught in a thicket by his horns:
> Offer the ram of pride instead of him.
> But the old man would not do so, but slew his son
> And half the seed of Europe, one by one.[1]

War, greed, prestige, vainglory—these take men to be expendable and set them on the altars of callousness and heed no warning voice. This power of man to immolate his own, to murder his blessings, to make of his dearest his victim, has to be known as a temptation halted unless it is to be a climax damned. On this level, Abraham's story, for all its context of sincerity, yields in focus the stern truth that only in turning aside is there salvation. It is when men believe themselves pursuing an absolute, whether perverse or plausible, that compassionate love is most urgent in its authority to interpose. To rejoice in its arresting, intervening cry against our own imagined ultimates is the deepest secret of Abraham. The deafness and blindness of those who do not hearken and turn are the tragic measure of their sin.

The transaction on Mount Moriah may thus be seen as a symbol of the furthest reach of man's existence and an index of the inclusiveness of his temptation. Man in Abraham is seen to stand at the centre of the paradox of good and evil. This is a story of the 'friend of God', and yet it holds within itself the elements of man's sharpest enmity to Him, the outlines of his highest presumption. By decisions other than Abraham's, Moriah becomes the shadow of the final defiance.

If, turning from that darkness into Abraham's light, we ask for

---

[1] *Collected Poems*, London, 1963, p. 42.

the sources of his conviction that he must 'offer' his son, it may be right to conjecture a sharp intensifying of his constant anxiety. Shall we understand, behind this dreadful errand, wood and knife in hand with Isaac, an inclusive crisis of apprehension in which he saw himself required to forgo his one hope? Is the whole event the single, traumatic experience of the precariousness of the 'seed', the jeopardy of the 'name'? Was he learning, in this dire manner, that he had his son and his hope, not by mere legal title, by dint of his own devising and protecting, but only by the—perhaps revocable—permission of God? Was the great lesson that he had Isaac only as a gift out of contradiction, that the circumstances of his birth were perpetuated in the miracle of his survival? Was he discovering how to depend on God, not on the gifts of God, and thus how to understand the totality of grace? Was the urgency of his fear so shattering that he found himself, as it were, compelled to do the worst with his own hands? *Periisem nisi periisem*, to borrow the motto chosen by Kierkegaard for his *Stages on Life's Way*: 'I had perished, had I not perished.' Returning from the land of Moriah there could be for Abraham no extremities of faith, no depths of despair, he had not already known and overcome. The Christian faith lives by similar convictions about the Cross of Christ.

It was not simply that Abraham had to face the bitter contingency of things. For he could have done so, and perhaps did, in some onset of plague or some natural calamity. Merely to know that Isaac might not survive would have needed no more than natural factors, threats in plenty from the external world of tempest and disease, and the human world of sword and malice. The crucial thing was being dramatized under his own hand, enacted by his own decision. The meaning, then, is beyond all mere contingency. Does it lie in the thought that the God-given must always be the God-reserved? Was Abraham on Moriah the first to know that we have the dearest things truly only when we have them significantly to what is beyond them in God Himself? The very belief in God is wanting its true reality if it cannot, or will not, face the non-survival of Isaac.

We take this theme further if we say that inwardly for Abraham the journey to Moriah means an encounter with the ultimate dereliction, an experience of God-forsakenness. For in Isaac, every aspect of the Divine promise is invested: in the son of promise the whole logic of Abraham's being is staked. We see him, as it were, learning a final readiness for a lost cause. The most precious hopes see themselves overborne and overcome within the very hands that hold and cherish them. Even the most sacred area of instrumentality to the Divine end has to be yielded to that end itself. Only so can Abraham learn to trust God *with* salvation as well as merely *for* it. Of the two acts of faith the latter is always the easier.

'From that time on', observed Kierkegaard, 'Abraham became old.'[1] The rest of the story has to do with testamentary provisions and epilogue events. It might be truer to say that 'from that time on, Abraham was complete'. He has come to know that son and heir and promise are not in themselves the 'answer', full dearly as he holds them. By accepting that they might not be, he receives them back again with the authenticity of a new creation, and he knows himself to be beyond all lesser roles in history 'the friend of God'.

Have we read too much into the enigmas or the purposes of an old story? 'In the mount of the Lord, it shall be seen.' *Jehovah Jireh*, not a known place-name but the sum of an event in the soul. 'God sees' and 'God is seen': Abraham knows in being known.

This reflection on the climax of Abrahamic meanings in the Bible plainly owes much to a Christian sympathy of mind. But the kinship is its own justification. All three monotheisms have been eager to 'possess' Abraham. The Hebraic, of course, does so in its own right and by its own descent. The Islamic and the Christian, for their respective reasons, have reached back to him, standing as he does beyond the Sinaitic covenant and the Mosaic order, to a time before the nationhood of his descendants. They have greeted him, as it were, as a 'solitary' before the time of great community. St Paul and Muḥammad have, perhaps strangely, in common, this awareness of a Divine relationship, on

[1] *Fear and Trembling*, Eng. trans. by Walter Lowrie, Princeton, 1941, p. 13.

the part of Abraham, which antedates the institution of the Torah. They have welcomed it as exemplifying, and so corroborating, their own independence of the Jewish reception of the law, whether, with St Paul, in the interests of his Gospel of justification, or, for Muḥammad, in the name of another repository of the Divine will.

These concerns with Abraham, however, reach their tenderest and closest character in this final sphere of his voluntary dispossession of Isaac. The Christian Gospel, in something of this same dimension, is constituted by the like readiness to let all go in gaining all. Here the seeming contrast between an Isaac rescued through the substitution of a ram and a Jesus for whom there was no reprieve,[1] should not obscure the inner parallels. We have to reckon with the critical difference of an external array of circumstances and choices conspiring to the death of Jesus. No outside wills bent on satisfaction are present in the Genesis story. But the inner meaning of the Moriah road is plainly paralleled, indeed intensified, in the prospect of Gethsemane. Messiahship, in like oblation of its hopes, has to let itself be crucified in order that it may be consummated. The inner meaning of that decision in the ministry of Jesus Himself is the very definition of the faith that takes its name from the designation He achieved in suffering, namely being the *Christ*, the *Messiah*.

There was about that decision, in its heroic making within the mind of Jesus, and as the essence in the active of His Sonship to God, the same ultimate criteria we have traced in the foregoing interpretation of the Abrahamic. Messiah's 'promise' might have been sought, as popular image supposed, by militancy and by nationalism, by reducing opposition and enforcing submission. But by those means the ultimate enmities of men would have been no more than suppressed or multiplied. Such a Messiahship would win only in superficial, even Pyrrhic, victory. The fulfil-

---

[1] The writer well remembers an occasion in Ogbomosho, Nigeria, when this question was put to him. See 'West African Catechism', in *The Muslim World*, Vol. 48, No. 3, 1958, pp. 237–47. The matter has naturally a great fascination for Muslims in view of the Muslim certainty that Jesus ought to be rescued.

ment of its ultimate vocation required the readiness to suffer. For without suffering there is no final overcoming of evil. Thus it was that Jesus accomplished the Messianic ends only by letting go the traditionally Messianic means: it is both these acts together, as one, which we have learned to recognize as the secret of our redemption in terms of the Christian Christ. What by the criteria of the zealots looks like a lost cause is in fact triumphing by taking that apparent defeat, in its whole shame and loneliness, as the condition and ground of the only victory it seeks—the only victory that suffices.

There is, of course, much else in the Christian possession of Abraham, but these things are the heart of them. Something at least of St Paul's vigorous emphasis on the principle of faith as exemplified in Abraham arises from equally assured rabbinic arguments that claimed him for a clear exponent of works. On the basis of Eccles. xliv. 20[1] and other passages, it was urged that Abraham had known the covenant of Sinai by anticipation and kept it prospectively. Thus his whole odyssey might be invoked as a prelude to the Torah and the Torah in community as the ultimate reward of Abraham. Antithetically, St Paul, with his eager yearning after an inner integrity such as the law had not bestowed, and reversing this position, was keen to take Abraham as precedent for his vital principle of obedience and against the meritoriousness which for him so bedevilled the Torah's people. Important in its own sphere, this controversy over Abraham can easily conceal a basic identity in the fact of his personal relation with God, believing indeed and 'working' in an activity of faith, relevant both to Torah and Gospel.

Certainly, in his positive appeal to 'faithful Abraham', St Paul is right in finding the pattern of justification. To proceed upon the reliability of God, whether in the call out of Haran, or the calling to Christ, is to 'justify' God, to prove His nature, to experience His reality, and this, in turn, is the 'justification' of

---

[1] 'He kept the law of the Most High and was taken into covenant with Him . . . therefore He assured him by an oath that the nations should be blessed in his seed.'

men. Taken beyond, but not in neglect of, the controversy the New Testament records, in Galatians and in Romans, the evangelical significance of Abraham is seen to consist simply in this posture of taking as true promise what is understood as the Divine word and, in proceeding, bringing it to pass. This is what, on the part of the man who would be Christian, faith does in response to the fact of Jesus as the Christ. It is, in its inward essentials, an Abrahamic thing. Likewise, the theme which is at the heart of that fact of Christ may be seen foreshadowed by the drama of a father and a son going on together, with the wood of sacrifice toward a rendezvous on a hill.

Here, then, in 'seed', 'standing' and 'sacrifice' are the elements in the significance of Abraham as they have come to be focused in the three great faiths that take him for their ancestor. They are not to be isolated rigorously: for they inter-penetrate the life of all three systems. Jewry knows well enough the robust city-founding qualities of the Islamic Abraham. Christianity with its Constantines, its power wielding, its state partnerships, is no stranger to the exercise of the will to prevail which marks the keen iconoclast. Judaism is more familiar than any with the necessity of suffering, the pain of fidelity. Nor is the perspective of endurance absent from the history of Islam, both original and recent. Nothing within the tradition of Abraham is missing from the communities that hold him in the first stirrings of their common history. Such is his authority, such the embrace of his image.

Yet, in broad character, it is possible to join the three strands of his patriarchal meaning with the primary emphases of Hebrew, Muslim and Christian religion. There is the 'seed' of the chosen people, the 'station' of the devoted doer of God's will, and the 'suffering' of the willing bearer of the cost of faithfulness. There is the ethnic instrument, the active campaign, the patient redemption. Pondering these, in discernible contrast but common ground, we see that they correspond with three dimensions of the privilege of man and belong with the elemental mysteries of race, of power and of pathos. The 'secretarie Abraham' is well so named. For here is all mankind's epitome. Man, in being man, begets and shares the family. Man, in living as man, strives and builds the city. Man, in knowing he is man, kneels and makes oblation. He is at once a creature of blood community, of political order and of finite mystery. In his responsible caliphate he moves among his kin, his works and his sorrows. We turn, seeking him, to the account of his empire as received in the common and distinctive understanding of the three communities of Abraham.

'How astonishing', wrote Herbert Spencer in his *Autobiography*, 'is the supposition that the Cause from which have arisen thirty million of suns, with their attendant planets, took the form of a man and made a bargain with Abraham to give him territory in return for allegiance.'[1] Agreed! it is astonishing. But perhaps we may come, at the end, to a different sort of astonishment than Herbert Spencer had in mind.

[1] London, 1904, Vol. i, p. 152.

IV

The Chosen and the Nations:
The Paradox of Jewish Humanity

'A WANDERING Aramean was my father: and he went down
into Egypt and sojourned there with a few, and became
there a nation . . . and the Lord brought us forth out of Egypt . . .
and into this place, and has given us this land' (Deut. xxvi. 5, 8–9).
Nomadism, immigration, emigration, territory, nationhood—all
are there in a summary of history and a personal liturgy given to
the worshipper for the presentation of his first fruits by the author
of Deuteronomy. A theology of wealth and an interpretation of
the past, it consecrates habitation in a confession of the relationships, both transient and possessive, between land and people. It
is, we might say, the poetry of faith giving voice to the self-
awareness of a nation as shaped in the movement of time and
endowed with the resources of nature. In the immediacy of his
own early harvest, the faithful son of Jacob joins himself, in the
words of his own law, with the patriarchal wanderings, contrasts
his security with their adventures and gathers past and present
into a single hallowing. Here, in characteristic accents, is the
Hebrew expression of the privilege of man. The aim of this
Chapter is to consider what the Hebraic makes of the human in
its bold, reverent, yet sharply particularizing, version of the
experience of life.

The essential clue is the quality of the nomad. The 'Syrian ready
to perish', as the Authorized Version runs, was Jacob, the wanderer
of Bethel, the struggler at Jabbok. But the phrase fits Abraham
equally well since he was bound up with the same kinship. How
wandering and faith belonged together in his story, as a careful
imagination might suggest, we have already seen. For all the
uniqueness of Abraham's stature, there is a continuing logic
through the whole sequence. The very phrase, 'the God of
Abraham, of Isaac, and of Jacob', sets the successor figures in the

same tradition. 'The desert as a metaphysical experience ... coloured all their evaluations.'[1] It is imperative to reckon with the deep significance of the geographical element in the whole development of Hebrew tradition and theology. The alternation of history between the desert and the sown, between the nomadic condition and the settled habitation of river cities or communities, is the profoundly formative factor in the Old Testament understanding of God. On either side of the sojourn in Egypt, in both the patriarchal and the wilderness history, it is the necessities and conditions of a wandering existence which explain the character of Biblical faith.

Perhaps the surest way to learn this secret is to take at the full, both before the entry and after the Exodus, the fascination of Egypt. For the Nile vetoes all wandering and, as its gift, Egypt, of all countries, dissuades the very notion of exodus. To live is to stay by the river: life is nothing if not gregarious. Fully to know the nomadic generations in religious terms one has to measure what Joseph meant by 'the good of all the land of Egypt' and what Moses did in forsaking it. It was a 'good' which nurtured not only a clinging population, but a static temper of mind. The Egypt of the Pharaohs was tributary to the imperious sun, indwelling the heavens and in majestic circuit through the underworld beneath the earth, in a diurnal rhythm of mystery and power. The sun rose in the east, slanting the fertile green of the river's vital flow from behind the eastern waste of scrub and thorn, to set in the west beyond the empty stretches of the desert. Lapped in this double divinity of nature, man was fashioned in non-heroic mould, pre-ordained, as it seemed, for a station of subjection. Nature gave all and demanded to receive all, with Pharaonic power as the earthly symbol and custodian of those exacting and enervating deities. There was comfort in the swelling of the Nile but no trespass, either physical or emotional, beyond her reach. The sun-god of the heavens was equally relentless in dominion.

[1] See H. and H. A. Frankfort, in *Reader in Comparative Religion*, edited by Wm. A. Lessa and Evon Z. Vogt, New York, 1965, p. 493.

It was, after all, a collapse of the shepherd life of Jacob's family that brought the old patriarch, in the wake of Joseph's tribulation and triumph, into Egypt. The history makes plain that it was precariousness which forced the fathers into the gates of Egypt and precariousness which awaited their emergence from them. When they 'went down' into Goshen they had already the strenuous sense of community and identity which was to carry them through centuries of exile from their traditional patterns of existence. That their Egyptian era finally terminated in cruel oppression was directly due to dynastic change. But that final subjugation emerges as a kind of symbol of the steady spiritual menace to their ruggedness of the ethos which regarded shepherds with disdain and in its own cultic bondage to sun and river had no mind for nomads' worship.

So it was that the climax of the Exodus itself both renews and re-inaugurates in larger terms the inner quality of the Hebrew faith in destiny, under a deity known in historical event, and moving through particular and decisive crises with his people. This is the actual matrix of the sense of chosenness—not an abstract *theory* of distinction, but a living, moving sequence of 'choosing' history, with new departures and vital initiatives, foreign indeed to the settledness of the Nile river and the Nile sky, but authentic enough to the temper of nomadic courage. In this living way all natural phenomena were, Biblically, subordinated to a Divine will, not rhythmically merged in their recurrence but spontaneously related to responsive human hopes and fears.

It is urgent to add that this does not mean the desacralization of the natural. On the contrary: the pageant and wonder of the recurring days, the power and awesomeness of winds and rocks and waters, the mysteries of fertility and harvest, are all the more hallowed and grateful realities. 'Sacred' history is not such to the exclusion of 'natural' history. How could it be? For every drama needs its stage and every event of the Biblical experience turns, essentially, on the physical reality of the external order, the wells, the seas, the volcanoes, the vineyards, the mountain peaks, the deserts of privation with bushes that burn and manna that falls. There could be no meaning to the conviction of significance in history unless nature were already capable of sustaining, and indeed affording, the occasions in which that destiny is read by the faith that undergoes its temporal means. Biblical theology has from time to time, and much of late, been sadly disserved by a foolish depreciation of the realm of nature.

Hebrew faith certainly believes itself alive to the Divine as always beyond and above nature. It learns the absolute transcendence of God. Sun and moon and river, and all else, are robbed by the meaning of experience of all divinization and all their attributes are powers of God alone. The courage of this inner iconoclasm is as great as the courage of adventure into Exodus by which it is expressed and energized. It is from these convictions of the supreme majesty of God, over all times, places and powers, that the sense of elected status, of peculiar vocation, comes. The one is the corollary of the other. The God whom all things serve is free for untrammelled purposes. One may even quit the sheltering Nile and be borne out of the womb of Goshen into the perilous life of the real Sinai, in the assurance of that faith; and in the going the faith itself is known for truth. The God of the Hebrews is at once *over* nature and yet working through it, in beneficence and power.

Election, so discerned, is emphatically a theology also of creation. They must be resolutely held together. This necessity is the more important in that some current writing, inspired in part by a technology complex and a secular intimidation, seems concerned to decry the natural dimension in the Biblical record and to magnify, against it, the notions of election and history. Thus, for example, von Rad, commenting on Genesis i and ii, avers: 'Faith in creation is neither the position nor the goal of the declarations in Genesis 1 and 2', and warns against the idea that, in view of 'the position of the creation story at the beginning of our Bible', the doctrine of creation might be taken to be 'a central subject of Old Testament faith'. This commentator continues:'. . . this preface (Genesis i) has only an ancillary function. It points the course that God took with the world until He called Abraham and formed the community.'[1] This is indeed an unhappy confusion of mind. The 'electability' of any race must surely be seen as a comment on the whole. If the sense of election, as Biblically articulate, means a taking into one's own racial being of the whole intention of creation, that is only rightly seen as justifying, not exclusifying, the human meaning. We must insist, with Biblical authority from prophet, psalm and Torah, that creation is *for* election only because election is *within* and subject to creation. Only so can we repudiate the folly and fallacy of a Divine favouritism. The importance of this distinction will recur below. Unless it is observed, we shall have relegated the whole Old Testament experience of history to the status of a private delusion. Only if what election means is essentially universal can it even historically stand. Can the interpretation of experience as election be authentic for any if it is not potential for all?

It is only with that assurance in view that we can turn intelligently and confidently to the mind of the Old Testament. There, pivoted on the Exodus, we find natural phenomena relative to a Divine Lordship and that Lordship historically proceeding in conjunction with a particular people. Or, conversely, we find a particular people responding to historical events in the context of natural phenomena as fulfilling and achieving with and for them the purpose of a Divine Lordship. The whole privilege of man in place and time is intensified in a single focus by a people who assume it to be uniquely their own. The assumption is, so to speak, the condition of the intensity. They participate, we might say, in humanity by differentiation from mankind.

INTO HUMANITY OUT OF MANKIND: THE FACT

Old Testament experience stands as a unique acceptance of the privilege of man, but only at the price of an ethnic distinction from the rest of mankind. In its greatness and its nemesis, this paradox makes for the profoundest irony of history. An intense

[1] G. von Rad, *Genesis*, trans. by J. H. Marks, 1961 (German edition, 1956), London, pp. 43–4.

vocation, in which we may read for all time what man is for, is exemplified and achieved only at the price of a studied, and essential, seclusion from the generality of the world. Humanity, in essential significance, moving and acting in time and territory, takes definition from a particular history. But the crux of the same history is an effective, and frustrating, exemption of mankind from the full measure of its meaning. The blessing and the curse belong together. The vision and the veto arise from the same context. An inclusive disclosure of the human dimension takes an exclusive character. Humanity is attained in Israel, but only by vital reservations of Israel from mankind. The history of Semitic religion as a whole has to do with the yearning to possess this human dignity and to dispossess the monopoly in which it had birth. Christianity and Islam, in their different ways, struggle to universalize the Hebrew definition of man. Judaism continues to see the particular as necessarily perpetuated. But this is to anticipate. Our immediate business is to see man, as man in Hebrew covenant is, before turning to the nemesis implicit in that fact that only Hebrew man was in it. The tragedy by which covenants exclusify is, in the end, the measure of the status they confer. The question of their limitation only arises in the context of their benediction. Where the Old Testament secret is not open, then the greater the violation in its preservation.

How symbolic that this whole issue should hinge historically on exodus! For nowhere is the story more poetically moving 'out of mankind into humanity'. This is the historical constitution of the nation, its emergence into conscious, corporate destiny under the leadership of Moses. He survives, as an infant born into oppressive captivity, because he is 'drawn out of the water'. He lives to draw out the people from the waters of affliction, from the waters of the Nile, from servitude and safety, from timid subjugation to Pharaoh's power exploiting the facts of geography to crush the hopes of life. In that crisis, as the sacred history takes it, lies the secret of the whole. The myth of the Nile's necessity, of Pharaoh's prescriptive right to tyranny, is broken. By a supreme adventure the people are liberated from a slow conspiracy of genocide by oppression, from all the bitternesses of hard bondage. They renew the temper of their patriarchal sagas and commit themselves to the wilderness, sealed by the closing waters of the Red Sea behind them, engulfing in one climax both their own victim-status and their tyrant's claim.

The magnitude of that transaction, first stirred into hope at the burning bush, is most surely measured in the question Moses himself then imagined the people asking, when he came to them with the summons to an exodus. 'When I say unto them: "The God of your fathers hath sent me unto you and they shall say to me: What is his name? What shall I say unto them?"' (Exod. iii. 14.) The familiar reply, usually given as: 'I am that I am', is, of course, no dubious enigma, no metaphysical evasion of an answer. For the question was in no way philosophical. Nor could it be answered by a puzzle. The anxious, urgent interrogative and the purport of the response belong together and must be so interpreted. Both, if the phrase may be permitted, are 'existential'. The people are asking, not for disquisition, but for authenticity. Frantic with mingled torture and aspiration, they want to know whether the only exchange for Pharaoh's whip is a lingering death in the waterless sand. Sick at once with despair and yearning, they ask about the integrity of this proposed celestial deliverer. Beyond Moses, as Moses well knew, they demanded the credentials of his supposed commissioner in heaven. The God of Abraham had, for barren decades, been singularly quiescent. What to historians might look like the providences of Joseph had come to seem to Moses' generation like a mocking deliverance of the hungry into the hands of the ruthless. What then was the character of this suddenly cognisant deity offering emancipation? The oppressed had fallen into that deepest of scepticisms that fears even hope itself. Moses had rightly gauged the mood of his listeners.

So had the reply he was directed to return. 'I will be there as he whom I there will be.' We must take the grammatical element of futurity as crucial to the meaning. The promise underwrites the dependability of the God of exodus only in the Exodus itself.

There are, and can be, no advance guarantees. Only in going through exodus in His keeping can the God of the promise be known. Nor can there be, by some 'revelation' of the 'Name', any authority over Him, any requiring of His word. The event alone substantiates both its veracity and His promise.

Here, once and for all, though in supreme drama, is the steadfast principle of Biblical revelation, namely that history is the point of encounter with truth. God is not the God of abstraction and rumination, but of action and trust. The fact of the Exodus takes the people of God decisively out of Egypt and in that sense out of mankind. For it gives them a distinctive experience through which they find incorporation. 'They were all baptised unto Moses in the cloud and in the sea', as St Paul has it (1 Cor. x. 2). They were facing, in most emphatic independence, the loneliness of a new and now 'national' nomadism, the solitariness of the desert before them, and with it and by it, the uniqueness of their destiny. Their departure from Egypt, in all the circumstances of miracle and reversal of 'fortune', could only be received and interpreted as a crisis of historical discrimination, in which for perpetuity their future had been bound together with the intention of God. In this conviction they resumed, as retrospect allows us to identify, the essential understanding by which they knew and revered their own ancestral heroes beyond the immigration of Jacob. The Joseph cycle of their history, so to speak, had come round full circle, ending for the whole, as it had begun for the one, in the 'iron in the soul'. Loosed from that torture, they were loosed also, as their traditions tell, from the crippling perplexity of their Egyptian anonymity before God mirrored in the very namelessness of God Himself.

This, of course, is to seize upon the inner logic of the heart of things. It is not to ignore the repeated frustrations of Moses, the frequent recalcitrance of the crowd. These were the outward tumults of the inward destiny. The covenant at Sinai took note of both. It epitomized the mystery within, by ordaining the discipline of the turmoil around. It turns the experience of the Exodus into the charter of relationship between the God of the Exodus and the people of the Exodus. As the great transaction of the wilder-ness it binds the purpose of their liberation with the promise of their territory. It establishes in Divine-human fidelities the mutual roles of God and people. 'I will be their God and they shall be my people.' There is through the whole concept of Torah this theme of co-operation, permeating the sense of the historical and of the economic. What has been and what is, the past out of which the generations came and the future for which they are made, have their significance in this inclusive direction, toward God and His will, of the exclusive identity which is the sense of Israel. They are a different people, as the Exodus allows none to doubt: the quality and obligation of their difference the Torah will define and ensure.

By these broad perspectives, the whole subsequent history is written and becomes the history in the writing. The factuality, as we saw with Abraham, is the interpretation. Events were of the sort to generate this acceptance of their meaning. There is neither place, nor need, here to explore the sequence in the story of the monarchy or to trace the vicissitudes of a long narrative. The presentation in the Old Testament doubtless reflects many cross-currents of stress and controversy and partisanship, not least in the Saul/Samuel conflicts. But the rule of the covenant is the definitive principle by which all else—husbandry, policy, state-craft, society and commerce—are adjudged. In the deep signi-ficance of the prophets in Israel the shape which the covenant gives to the human standing comes into its most intense and eloquent expression. They are, we may say, the spokesmen of the God of hope. Their appeal to their people goes back into the creative, beyond the elective, order. It embraces both the soil and the soul of the people. It takes the land seriously as possessed through the drama of the history but instinct also with the beauty and dependability of its ordered processes.

The 'controversy' in which the great prophets engage with their hearers never deviates from the trust of 'a land flowing with milk and honey . . . whose stones are iron' and whose hills yield brass, 'a land for which the Lord cares'. But it is a trust which does not merely consist in a physical occupancy, an ancestral residence, with no sense of decisiveness in history. It is, by contrast, a land which might never have been possessed had there not been a compassion that wrought to make it such and to make it theirs. In these terms, the prophets married together the intimacy and earthboundness of the pagan cults they struggled to suppress with the sublime authority of the lordship over history known in their people's stature.

Just as the creative 'Let there be . . .' subdued to order the chaos of 'the deep', so there is a sort of co-imperative with it in the 'Thou shalt . . .' at Sinai. The one calls into being, the other into obedience. The material of the second, however, is unlike the first. It is not nature and the physical, but man and the volitional. More precisely, it is Hebrew man taking upon himself the definitive human charter and hallowing his posture towards it by the sanction of uniqueness among peoples. It is as if the human vocation is too precious to be shared, too crucial to be general, too great a privilege for the unprivileged.

But, for all their readiness to measure up for man to manhood, Hebrew humanity is far from docile and submissive. On the contrary, their history is punctuated with crises of disloyalty and these, in turn, are both the context and the necessity of the prophetic role. In changing circumstances, through every generation and out of every distortion, the vocation of the people of God must be perpetually renewed. Through the prophets the law scrutinizes men's hearts and re-iterates its claims. It reproves and chastens through their interpretation of its meaning in the current of events and through their stern and costly persistence in its relevance. The whole sequence of the prophets on the behalf of Torah may be seen as the unremitting, invincible hope of God, never abandoning humanity, never acquiescing in their perversity and never reciprocating their neglect of Him.

One central theme within that sustained service of prophecy to the law is the periodic reproach of priesthood as the other dimension of the human order under God. 'A kingdom of priests' was the classic phrase denoting the whole people, called to the hallowing of their seedtime and their harvest, invited to the steady, grateful recognition of God in the simplicities of an agrarian existence and the happy cycle of fertility. Not only were there here the temptations of a pagan, cultic pluralism, the *baals* and their pitfalls: there were also the typical religious temptations of priestly formalism and of ritual office. Hebrew religion, for all its uniqueness, was in no way immune from the subtle distortions whereby the very recognition of the Divine may become a studied evasion of God and of His claims. Prophecy itself, in a comparable way, was capable of becoming professional and merely sanguine, of lending its forms to political expediency or moral compromise.

But these issues are to be seen as a measure of the wilfulness of man, perverting even the instruments of a true righteousness, whether in the sanctuary or the market, to the distortion of their character, the prostitution of their trust. Indeed, this very metaphor of a ruptured loyalty in love is frequent among the prophets. But, whatever the imagery, the Biblical history in its long, uneven sequence, sees the covenant as in constant tension with recalcitrance. Prophets are flouted and destiny is betrayed. Estrangement mars and refuses the conditions of the Divine fellowship. The land is alienated from its due and sacramental meaning under men's hands. Exile, foreseen by true prophets, comes finally as the counter-climax to the Exodus and the proper symbol of a chapter closed in a destiny unfinished. 'How shall we sing the Lord's song in a strange land?'

With exile and disenlandisement wholly new dimensions are added to the Hebrew experience of being human. It is now a far different bitterness from the Egyptian sojourn of the fathers. The tragedy is not now that of simple privation and a silent heaven, but of forfeiture and self-inflicted undoing. Even in their wretchedness by 'the waters of Chebar', the exiles are still in a strange apartness from the generality of men. Human adversity, it is true, has an inescapable quality of potential kinship within it, as part of the finitude which belongs to all. The expatriate lot of the Hebrew exiles certainly brought them into realms of thought and usage, hitherto unknown, which came powerfully to affect their temper and theology. Some of their number, moreover, acquiesced in the Babylonian world and reconciled themselves to a dispersion in the physical abandonment of Zion. But these things notwithstanding, the exiles retained and fostered the irreducible conviction of a Hebrew privacy with God, of which a territorial return for the more ardent among the émigrés could be the only sign and satisfaction.

The entire cycle of events in this passage of Jewish history, the inevitable abeyance of the Temple, the new 'synagogue' form of the centrality of the Law, and the ever more crucial task of the prophets, served to bring home the conditionality of the covenant. The tempting notion, so prevalent before the heroic exclusion of it by Jeremiah, that there was some conditionless immunity of Jerusalem from invasion and disaster was decisively disqualified. The central illusion of the people of God that Zion was inviolate, fortified in many hearts by the lengthy survival of Judah beyond the collapse of the northern kingdom, was finally discredited. The traumatic effect of this discovery remained with the soul of Jewry through all succeeding struggles for its recovery. All subsequent efforts to renew the territorial reality of Zion, whether wistful and dogged as under Haggai, or intense and fierce as with the Maccabees, lay under the irresistible logic of that catastrophe of 586 B.C. Zedekiah's tragic end had confirmed most tellingly the patient fidelity and costly truth-bearing of the loyal prophets whose tenacity through travail paved the way for the genesis of the new covenant. It sustained their valiant perception of the truth that covenantal election is an inward crisis, that history is judgement because it is mercy.

It is, therefore, in the prophetic religion, as the Exile learns and releases it, that, paradoxically, the Old Testament attains its most magnificent expression of the dignity of man. These writers, these 'servants of the word', are beyond all illusions of temporal prosperity. By their rejection of the false securities of statecraft, their readiness for the courageous bearing of contumely and the hostility of false and easy nationalists who call them traitors, they bear in their own persons the travail of a genuine humanity. They refuse to promise security where God offers only crisis, and by their sufferings they give the lie to voices that preach patriotism as an end in itself. In this quality they carry, as we must see, the seeds of an emancipation from the deceits of misconstrued election. Here, as in many other of its themes, the Old Testament is the best source of its own indictments.

It is, nevertheless, the tragic irony of Hebrew history that these, the truest, mentors of the vocation of the whole people of God are, for the most part, silenced or despised. The figure of the suffering servant who emerges with such patient authority from within these prophetic dimensions of perception is the *suffering* servant. With Messiahship in Jesus as its surest sequel and fulfilment, the significance of the suffering servant reaches its ultimate term. In and from that climax, as the Christian spirit and faith have taken it, unrecognized or disavowed as it is in Jewry, the irony deepens even further. For continuing into Christian history, in the form and in the terms of Messiah crucified, the prophetic Hebrew conviction becomes universally accessible but is at the same time disallowed that fruition by its own heirs. In turn, as all history knows, the Christian institution in the world becomes a new factor in the isolation and separateness of the Jews—an apartness later powerfully, if differently, reinforced by the energies and postures of Islam as, in effect, a new sort of Sinai in Arabia.

The intensest experiences of the Hebrew spirit are, then, a profound measure of the stature and meaning of man, deserving to be universal in their relevance yet somehow always constituted in, and provocative of, seclusion from the rest of men. The barest sketch of this paradox, against the background of interpreted history from Abraham to Jesus, does no sort of justice to the sharp complexities and tangled vicissitudes of the story. It could not propose to do so. Our concern has been simply to state the fact, to follow the Hebraic into the human, to test and learn the definition given to man by the self-awareness of Israel and to observe how at every point its deepest perception of what it is to know blood-unity, to savour sorrow, to possess territory, to remember history, to dream dreams, to hold faith and to give thanks—all intensely human realities—is fused with the splendid yet frustrating conviction that the perception is unique and the experience exclusive and exclusifying. The Old Testament leaves mankind out, in order to participate in man. Other men and nations are the foil of its own identity. Yet its identity has to become the clue to all.

INTO MANKIND IN THIS HUMANITY: THE QUESTIONS

Are not these seclusions of the Hebraic, it will be asked, the natural and inescapable condition of *any* identity? Can there be human expression without irreducible denominators of race, birth, land, ancestry, tradition and history? Is it not likewise with all peoples, that they know themselves, in these human elements, by contradistinction from other peoples, in other lands, by other births, with other tongues? Ought we to reproach the Jewish for some peculiar awareness of peculiarity? Can there be any human which is not also a particular?

The point is well taken. Self-awareness is identity-awareness. Being is being somebody and the elements that are central to Hebraic existence are constitutive anywhere of peoples and communities. Just as power, when we come to Islam, is inseparable from life, so race and birth are. The issue, in both cases, however, is not with the physical actuality but the religious interpretation. It is the emotional and theological intensification of the denominator into election and covenant, into a kind of 'we only' of the spirit, which is the real paradox and the crucial problem. It is the religious quality given to the equations of place and time and 'seed', which makes the exclusifying character more than a circumstance and erects it into a creed and a spiritual seclusion.

There are broadly two questions which concern us here. The one is the dilemma of the means that have overcome the end, the paradox by which the instrument has become the absolute. The other is the reversal of this self-possession of election by a genuine and effectual fulfilment of universality.

Election in its deepest expression in the Old Testament is

deliberately purposive. It is only to service and for the world. Abraham is presented in the history as the ancestor whose benediction will reach all nations. 'The nations shall come to thy light' is the prophet's understanding of the vocation of Israel in the great age of prophetic achievement. Amos, too, is able to discern in the movements of other tribes and nations in history the outworking of the purpose of God. Yet the fascination of the elective status tends throughout to become an end in itself, and what is meant to be always relative, to ends beyond itself, becomes absolutized as a good that needs no goal to justify its status. This process can always be explained as the necessary preservation of the vital instrument. The service of the cause becomes so to speak the cause to be served. The ethnic gives itself an ultimacy which only properly belongs to the universal it was designed to serve.

This, of course, is the temptation of all vocation and we shall find the same situation within Islam over the instrumentality of power and the state. It is, in essence, the problem of 'hierarchy' within man's being. Community in birth, so emphatically epitomized in Jewry, is plainly a constituent of existence requiring and receiving, with more or less intensity, a dominating loyalty. To see that loyalty religiously, as the Old Testament does, is to place it firmly *under* the more ultimate and final loyalty due to God Himself. The dogma and experience of election and covenant intend and enshrine precisely that subordination. They give to it the sanction and authority of an absolute vocation. Islam does no less with its own concept of *Dīn* and *Daulah*, of religion *cum* empire. Yet it is just this quality of agent for the higher end that gives to Jewishness a presumption of ultimacy in and for itself. Making of race a religious thing, as chosenness does in Israel, contains this inner contradiction. It hallows and obligates community in birth as purposive for the Divine Lordship to which it must subdue all its will and wealth. Yet in this very context it allows, even encourages, that end-beyond-itself-conviction to justify and sustain an aggressive self-protection and, over against other peoples, a proud superiority. This is the paradox which all the history underlines. The end is captured by the means. The religious dimension which ought to bestow the benediction of disciplined fulfilment spells, in fact, a more subtle corroboration of self-interest and assertion.

History, of course, is full of examples on various levels of this central paradox of religion, the conviction of Divine relation to obviate the fact of it, the use of God to elude God, the service of heaven in the interests of men. But there is a pathos and a depth about the Jewish exemplification of it that are unique and haunting. The humanist and the secularizer, no doubt, would scorn and dismiss it altogether. Better a frank, uncomplicated human ultimacy, shorn of both the sanctions and the temptations of the religio-racial, the religio-political, or the religio-moral, complex. At least, then, the workings of human nature are freed from the emotions and hypocrisies that go with any transcendent reference. But that way lies the other and larger devil of untrammelled absolutism, the menace to the human situation of a repudiation of any final obligation. That God may be selfishly invoked only emphasizes the more sharply the urgency with which we need to find Him truly. We are not honest with the temptations of religion if we take them as the only possibility. Unless they can be transcended they are not perversities to blame.

Two related queries may have suggested themselves in the foregoing. Is Jewry really so 'racial' a phenomenon as the argument apparently assumes? And is it well to pose the large problem of religious 'sanctions' so squarely in Old Testament terms as if the Hebrew tradition was the sole, or even the supreme, example of the relative made absolute? The answer to the first is complex. It is clear that one cannot explain the mystery of Jewishness in history on ethnic grounds alone. But one certainly cannot explain it and ignore them. The further we move, of course, from origins into the endless migrations, vicissitudes, and sequences of Jewish history in diaspora, the more enigmatic and tremendous their diversified identity becomes. It is plainly constituted by many elements, while denominators vital in most other historical identities, land, speech, state, and the rest, are seen to be dispensable in the miracle of Jewish continuity. Yet, for all the diversification, there remains in genesis and in essence this governing notion, this definitive reality of 'the seed of Jacob'. In the origins that give history its amazing impetus, election, as we have argued, is rooted in an ethnic experience of common deliverance, of common Torah-trust, of common enlandisement, and of common ancestry. The long centuries have brought attenuation of the racial element in its merely physical sense. But ideologically it abides as the determinative factor in the self-understanding of 'the chosen *people*'. 'All our fathers' is not a confession of genealogy but of a holy incorporation. It is ethnic by virtue of its theology.

Turning to the second query, there are surely broad grounds for regarding the Hebrew thesis of distinctiveness as the most insistent and crucial in all history. It is, therefore, entirely fitting to see in it the most fundamental reckoning with the conscious-ness of identity and, for that reason, to take it as an eloquent test-case of human privilege through birth into community. All other 'tribalisms', it might be said, can find their fullness in this one. Hebrew election is *par excellence* the assurance of history with us, of geography for us, of God through us. Within its own and for its own, it gives to the sense of 'we-ness' the profoundest and most telling assurance, combining Divine significance with com-munal awareness in the closest relation. It constitutes the most convinced theology of being a people and is, therefore, foremost in its sense of obligation for what it is and in tenacity in being it.

For both reasons it has aroused the strongest antipathies. From the beginnings of its 'national' history, the events and interpreta-tions achieving and confirming its chosenness have been com-petitive. The Exodus was necessarily the discomfiture of Pharaoh. Joshua and Jericho, Deborah and Sisera, Samuel and the Amale-kites—these are the antitheses which litter the story. The circum-cised know themselves in their scorn for the uncircumcised: the law is esteemed in the context of 'the lesser breeds' outside it. The psalmist instinctively, and frequently, identifies his enemies with God's and righteousness with their defeat. Even yet, in some

quarters, the Old Testament provides a useful quarry for philosophies that reduce the alien peoples to 'hewers of wood and
drawers of water'. The price of distinctiveness is distinction and
all too readily the sense of the Divine favour here becomes the
certainty of a Divine enmity there.

The Hebrew genius showed itself splendidly capable of surmounting such antipathies and taking only the positive, without
the negative, meanings of election. Then there is no finer school
than the universalism of the Old Testament in which to learn the
inclusive view of mankind.

It is too light a thing that you should be my servant to raise up the
tribes of Jacob and to restore the preserved of Israel: I will give you as
a light to the nations, that my salvation may reach to the end of the
earth.[1]

Psalm 87 sees Zion as the one mother of the nations:

> Babylon and Egypt I will count among those that know
> me; Philistia, Tyre, Ethiopia, these will be her
> children and Zion shall be called 'Mother,'
> For all shall be her children.
> It is He, the Lord most High, who gives each his place.
> In his register of peoples he writes:
> 'These are her children.'
> And while they dance they will sing:
> 'In you all find their home.'[2]

This welcome to the generality of mankind, even to nations of
traditional hostility, arose from the larger contemplation of history, from reflection on the common elements of life, from the
deep, moral personalism of the greatest prophets. It was in debt,
also, to the influences of the post-exilic experience and of the
Greek temper. Thus, in the Book of the Wisdom of Solomon:

When I was born, I began to breathe the common air, and fell upon
the kindred earth, and my first sound was a cry, like that of all. I was
nursed with care in swaddling clothes. For no king has had a different

---

[1] Isa. xlix. 6 (R.S.V.).
[2] Quoted from the Gelineau version.

beginning of existence; there is for all mankind one entrance into life, and a common departure.[1]

This embrace of common mortality, this incorporation into all, did not diminish the conviction of particular purpose but gave it humility and openness.

Yet history did not stay in these dimensions. For a variety of reasons, perhaps in part because the Christian faith institutionalized this universal promise of the Hebrew vision and in so doing frightened Jewry into new forms of privacy, the tragic pattern has persisted. In the broad perspective of history Jewish election and Gentile alienation perpetuate a mutual tension and antipathy. There is no occasion here for even the scantiest summary of centuries and the long windings of the story, through seclusion, rejection, bigotry, massacre, accommodation, assimilation, concord, conflict and recrimination.[2] In the throes of persecution, the Jew found himself appealing to the common humanity his traditional religious privacies had left behind.

Hath not a Jew eyes: hath not a Jew hands, organs, dimensions, senses, affections, passions? fed with the same food, hurt with the same weapons, subject to the same diseases, healed by the same means, warmed and cooled by the same winter and summer, as a Christian is? If you prick us, do we not bleed? If you tickle us, do we not laugh? If you poison us, do we not die? and if you wrong us, shall we not revenge?[3]

Shakespeare did not know in the end what to do with Shylock. Even his genius could not bring forth a climax to the trial scene worthy of the warped greatness of its victim. The fates were too heavily loaded, the legal fiction too cheap, the Gentile advantages too evident. Shylock moves too abjectly from defiance and cunning into brokenness and despair. His devices, from one angle, forfeit all claim to justice and blunt all but the most strong compassion. He has no right to anything better than to have his bond

---

[1] Wisd. of Sol. vii. 3–6 (R.S.V.).

[2] See, for example, Jabob Katz, *Exclusiveness and Tolerance, Studies in Jewish-Gentile Relations in Medieval and Modern Times*, Oxford, 1961.

[3] *The Merchant of Venice*, III. i.

and his malevolence cheated of their prey. His viciousness earns only the retaliation of the world that had evoked it, and somehow in their savagery both seem justified, short of forcible conversion —though even here a dominant society might plead a certain rough efficiency of self-protection, as long as Shylock holds against it the threat of a sharp usury that will not practise commerce. Yet commerce is in effect denied him since he cannot mingle. It is the world around that has made Shylock what he is; but how far has what Shylock is required this of the world?

Shakespeare's play has the whole tragedy of Jewry, and that all the more tellingly for the ambient comedy of Gentile lightheartedness and suavity. 'A man more sinned against than sinning', Shylock was, truly. Yet has he not provoked his prey to prey on him? If his is the greater provocation, where in the depths of history does the provoking derive? Human relations contain no more foul and desperate evil than Anti-Semitism. Has this to be the price, within the human scene, of 'chosenness' in the identity of one of its communities? 'Semitism', too, is unique in history or, better, Jewishness. Are we left, in the end, with the shattering irony that history's most intense sense of corporate religious destiny and its bitterest crime of rejection go together? Why has *this* election experienced *this* enmity? Why is it that Jewry has somehow become the butt of the deepest revelations of human perversity and Jewish existence somehow the touchstone of human antipathies? Is it that humanity cannot 'allow' so confidently 'elected' a people? How is that being a people on behalf of God has meant, so largely, being a people in spite of men? And what, through all the vexing tangle of these questions, becomes of the goal for which election stood, or stands?

Our concluding concern here is with that final question. It takes the deeper, metaphysical themes from which it springs, and for which no answers can be suggested here, into the realm of the practical. If it is agreed that the conviction of 'the chosen people' must find vindication in its meaning for all the nations, if its integrity hinges on its universal relevance, then two necessities would seem to be imperative. The first is that 'election' become a thesis of identity open to all peoples: the second is that it be grounded, finally, beyond the 'national' and the collective, in the personal as, in the final reckoning, its only feasible realm. The two aspects plainly inter-depend.

Every people is a chosen people. Territory, habitat, history, language and other denominators of community, however diversified, unequal, contrasted, have at least the common quality of causing identity to be. There may be great disparities between arid steppes and lush pastures, between arctic cold and tropical humidity. But in some measure the partnership and comradeship of soul and scene are universal. History, too, if you have the right historians, is capable of yielding mysteries of survival and adventure, sanctioning the sense of destiny. What, in Hebrew hands, evokes the assurance of uniqueness is discernibly potential in every collective continuity. The vital factor, finally, is not nature, or history, or territory, or climate: it is rather the will to believe. Israel's election, we may say, consists in the conviction of it. The God of choosing is the God of the chosen.

May we then find a way of emancipation from the oppressive and frustrating entail of Hebrew isolation by seeing the awareness of 'the people of God' as an education of all nations in how they might see themselves? Can we not claim it as transferable—a lesson in the will to exist instrumentally towards God and responsibly towards mankind? Such a view means no diminution of the Hebrew mystery. On the contrary, it invites all other peoples to enter into their own. It does not impugn the historic uniqueness of Jewry as in fact a supreme school of monotheistic faith: it merely refuses to see that uniqueness as jealously exclusive. It rather confirms and hails the one secret by proposing it to all. Unless the gist of 'election' is to be its withholding, unless its significance consists eternally in being unilateral—in which case the travesties abide and the resentments persist—then surely its destiny is realized in imitation. Judaism then fulfils itself in the tuition of the peoples in the calling to be a servant unto God.

Doubtless the same pitfalls await the wider acceptance of such Hebraic criteria of the ethnic experience within the privilege of man—pitfalls clear enough in the history of Jewry. Indeed, nations have often, already, incurred them. For there is nothing novel in the concept of nations 'Hebraicized'. Destiny in the Russian mind has frequently found expression in comparable terms to these. We have, perhaps, time for a wildly lyrical passage in this vein by Herman Melville on the United States:

Escaped from the bondage, Israel of old did not follow after the ways of the Egyptians. To her were given new things under the sun. And we Americans are the peculiar, chosen people, the Israel of our time: we bear the ark of the liberties of the world. Seventy years ago we escaped from thrall: and besides our first birthright, embracing one continent of the earth, God has given to us, for a future inheritance, the broad domains of the political pagans ... God has predestined, mankind expects great things from our race: and great things we feel in our souls.[1]

A draught of heady wine! But the crucial thing is that, whatever the exhilaration, it is subordination that is meant. The mastery that can be greeted in these exuberant terms is the one subdued to obligation. There is no eluding the realities of power, whether power enjoyed, or power forfeited. It is well that either circumstance should be sobered by responsible vocation. All we are concerned to argue is that the Hebrew understanding may be seen to suggest, for all nations, a clue to being themselves. The Old Testament faith has to do essentially with the ethnic dimension, with the business of nationhood. As such, it may be invoked to yield for all communities in blood or power, a pattern of identity at once secure and significant. And, if allowed this universal relevance, its own private meaning is surely the more fulfilled.

In all this, however, there is a further logic. The deep inner transition from the Old to the New Testament is a movement from the nation to the person. The former, of course, continues in relative covenantal possibility. But the crucial factor in the Divine economy comes to be 'holy and humble men of heart' in

[1] Herman Melville, *White Jacket*, New York, 1850, p. 189.

their individual fidelity rather than the nation in any corporate and collective standing.

The seed of this personal, and therefore universal, ground of righteousness derives from the old covenant itself. Within the heredity nature of the law's people deriving from Sinai, there had always been in every generation the problem of the obdurate 'son of the law', the man born within the covenant who, nevertheless, dishonoured it. From one angle, there never was, or could be, a disloyal Jew. For every Jew born was in full physical continuity with the elect people. Yet history abounded with renegades in spirit and in conduct. The idea of a whole people, uniformly and integrally responsive, as a nation, to the Divine will, proved a magnificent dream. It was a profound 'myth' of the soul, worthy in its aspiration to control the destiny and gird the hope of a whole people. It remains a stirring measure of the human privilege. But in actuality it could never be the truth of the masses. Was there not at the very foot of Sinai the obscenity of the golden calf?

Israel's history steadily and cumulatively illustrated the impracticality of an ethnic wholeness, of a particular society coterminous with human rightness and Divine reign. It had to be broken open to concede the insider's self-exclusion and to welcome the outsider's inclusion. The issue may best be taken where it finds its climax, namely in the experience and vocation of the greatest prophets. These heroic figures in the history of revelation moved, by their very calling, in a compelling awareness of *personal* identity. 'The Lord took *me* . . . and said: Go, prophesy . . .', declared Amos, dissociating himself from the professionalism of the soothsayers and grounding his authenticity in an inner transaction of his own heart. With Jeremiah, still more insistently, we encounter this note of urgent, autobiographical realism. The very recipience of the prophetic message means a vital intensification of individual character, engagement and capacity. Vocation means the fullest stretch of conscious, mental and spiritual power, all in a strenuously personal context.

This personal dimension is even more central in the crises of the preaching to which the prophetic calling leads. These call increasingly for a brave independence of mind in the service of unpopular truth. Only with steady, even defiant, courage can the recalcitrance of the masses be confronted and denounced. The prophets find themselves in a deepening minority-situation, until, as with Jeremiah, we find a single protagonist facing a nation-wide apostasy. Out of such tragic experience of lonely fidelity the germ of the new covenant is born, a covenant, not with the collective but with the individual, not with the ethnic but the responsive. By the same practical disqualification of the criterion of the nation the universalism which is indifferent to race or heritage can ultimately spring. As we have seen, the elimination of the notion of an inviolable Zion works to the same goal. The prophets teach their hearers to yearn in the midst of disaster for the law 'written in the heart'. For only in the faithful soul, not in citadels and sanctuaries, is the inviolable place.

Eloquent in the same sense is the fact that we neither find, nor somehow expect, in the supreme Biblical prophets a dependence on the political arm. Some are advisers or consultants, or more likely reprovers, of kings. They may speak politically. But they never hand themselves over to the political. There are none who take over the government. Herein is their surest relativizing of the nation. The will of God must always stand above the political and the collective and prophecy must reserve freedom of action and of accusation, over against the state, in a way that, identified with national interest, it never could.

This, in turn, is the source of their fundamental personal insecurity. Prophecy, as climaxed in Jeremiah, becomes 'perpetual pain'. We shall see more of this inescapable logic of new covenant in Chapter VI below. Here, it is plain on every score, that both the nature and the task of prophecy point to a ground of Divine relationship with men which, without abandoning the sphere of the collective, transcends it, and sets an ultimate reckoning with mankind, not in the womb of a people, but in the heart of a man.

How re-assuring it is to find the cogency of the new covenant emerging so emphatically from the experience of the old. It means that mind and spirit may respond to its liberating realism, with grateful indebtedness, as well as supersession, vis-à-vis the old. Through all the tragedies of Jewish particularism in history, and despite all the enmities into which 'the Gentiles' have been by stubbornness provoked, the paradox of the Hebraic vision of its own humanity yields these two abiding themes of tried experience, namely to take 'national' identity as vocation, and to discover that the trust of it passes out of that privacy into the universal and the human.

V

Apostolic Rule:
The Dilemma of Islamic Humanity

BIBLICAL vocabulary has a rare word which might perhaps be considered a precise, literal opposite of the Quranic word *muslim*. It is the Greek *sklērotrachēlos*, used in Stephen's speech in Acts vii and by the Septuagint in translating the six occasions in Exodus and Deuteronomy from which he was quoting.[1] The exact English equivalent is 'stiffnecked'. But we take it much more vividly if we set it, as we may, in contrast to the whole posture of Muslim prayer, with its deeply significant prostration, where the brow of man's pride, reverently brought to the earth, lays down all such unyielding arrogance in the humble fealty of worship.

To enjoin and ensure this true recognition of God was, of course, the central purpose of Muḥammad and Islam, and accordingly the 'stiffneckedness' of an insubordinate humanity was again their crucial theme and burden. The call of the Qur'ān confronted essentially the same problem as the Torah. Its Prophet was faced with his own dimension of the perennial dismay and sorrow which human obduracy created for the spokesmen of God in Israel. The whole meaning of the Law was its summons to men to recognize the directive will of God and to answer in full co-operation. But when, in their waywardness, they refused to do so, the Law's great mouthpiece, Moses, did not stay quiescently in the realm of words and exhortations. On the contrary: he entered upon new and resolute chapters of that leadership which from the beginning had been the context of the Torah's education of his people. He harnessed a vigorous initiative to concert the conformities his witness affirmed. There had been before him,

[1] Acts vii. 51, and Exod. xxxii. 9 and xxxiii. 3 and 5; and xxxiv. 9, and Deut. ix. 6 and 13.

and were after him, as Martin Buber notices, 'powerless and officeless' prophets from Heaven. But Moses

... though sent from above as they are, is sent not merely to speak, but also to perform: he is the commissioned leader of Israel ... The stern and deep realism of Moses ... determines the type, the order, of power ... in the hands of the 'charismatic leader' who is led by God; and for that very reason, this wielder of power must not engage in any transformation to dominion which is kept for God alone.[1]

'Not merely to speak, but also to perform ... the dominion ... kept for God alone'—the parallel, in both senses, between the Mosaic and the Islamic is unmistakeable. Muḥammad's mission, likewise, passes into rule and *imperium*, in face of the resistance that defies his words. Loyalty to his commission, as he sees it, carries the messenger beyond the pleas and warnings into the actions and policies by which rejection can be countered and subdued. The resulting structure of apostolic empire, of authority in instrumental relation to truth, makes Islam the focal expression of the fundamental 'political' problem of religion and the 'religious' dimension of politics. Through all this large territory of history and theology we encounter the same issue of the relative role and the absolute danger, which we have pondered in the 'ethnic' figuration characteristic of Jewry and Judaism. In the Muslim realm, however, the issue belongs, not primarily with a consciousness of ethnic identity and vocation, but instead with the theme and exercise of power.

The latter clearly has its ethnic elements. The vigour and thrust of Islam owe much, in their genesis and history, to the sense of an Arabic Qur'ān, *via* an Arab prophet, proceeding with an Arabian Caliphate. There is a deep, new solidarity about Islamic beginnings and a deliberate independence of earlier precedents, however formative, and existing faiths, however relevant. It would

[1] See Martin Buber, *Moses*, London, 1946, p. 87. He adds that this 'empowering' of the religious message tends, even against its will, to foster the popular association of authenticity with success. The fact that God is then identified with what prospers makes for a very serious disservice of religion. Thus Buber anticipates what is our main puzzle below.

be idle to ignore the urgent 'Arab' concerns in the rejection of the other 'peoples of the Book' and the Arabicization of their germinal example in the recipience of the Qur'ān. But, thanks to its universalism, and to other factors, it is not finally in this ethnic sphere that we can rightly locate the genius and essence of Islam. The quest for that central clue must take us, undoubtedly, to the dimension of organized community equipped with the sinews of strength. While Jewry, as it were, 'ethnicizes' its ultimate ground and sanction, in the idea and ideal of 'chosenness', Islam 'politicizes' them in the invocation of statehood as the surety and climax of the faith.

But the decision has the same paradox just traced in the heart of 'ethnic election', namely the trend towards an absolutism of that very element whose valid role is always instrumental. The crucial end of what, in concept, is relative, tends to preclude, in practice, its proper subordination as a means, until, the service forgotten, the instrument has become itself an ultimate. Or, in Buber's phrase, 'transformation into the dominion . . . kept for God', presents itself as a temptation within the very 'wielding of power'. Yet when, as before, we sense and question this inversion, the light by which we do so is the one we possess from those we think we inculpate. We learn to hope differently from them only by the categories which they have taught us. It is only from their confession of authentic instrumentality that the observer discerns the reckoning they intend. As with Jewish particularism, so with Islamic rule, the criterion of its criticism is its own. It cannot be relevantly judged before it is rightly approved.

The political embodiment of faith so characteristic of Islam is, by the same token, the crux of the Islamic understanding and acceptance of the privilege of man. There is no problem here such as we found earlier constituted for Jewry over the priority as between 'creation' and 'election'. Is the earth for the sake of Abraham or Abraham for the sake of the earth? 'Sacred history' there is in the Qur'ān, but not in the proprietary senses relished by some interpretations of the Old Testament. The central, historical interests of the Qur'ān are moral and didactic. It sees

earlier peoples, exemplifying, by their obedience or their dis-
obedience, the conditions of Divine favour or requital. There the
patriarchs are basically and essentially all prophets. The teleology
of history is not peculiar destiny but cumulative judgement and
the corroboration of Divine justice. Precisely because it transcends
the 'ethnic' and sees prophets sent to a variety of peoples and
prophecy itself culminating in a final and universal messenger,
but in the same inclusively educative and directive, rather than
redemptive or regenerating, relation to mankind, Islam has no
cause to perpetuate the Hebrew 'discrimination' of one land and
one people, over against other lands and other peoples. It does not,
in that way, particularize its theology of the economic order or
require its sense of history and of ecology to be dominated by an
'elected' perpetuity of uniqueness. Its horizons are, therefore,
open for a general, ethical, hortatory discipline for the human
tenancy of the good, or the indifferent, earth, sanctioned, however, and firmly undergirded, by the revealed authority of
government on behalf of God.

We have already sufficiently noted in Chapter II the Quranic
theology of the good of nature, its sense of 'signs' of God in the
natural order, addressing and engaging men's interest, intelligence,
gratitude and wonder. Precisely because of the absence of the
Hebraic dimension of particular election, there is all the greater
emphasis on what is generically human, on man as husband and
husbandman, on the life of tent and town, of oasis and family, of
commerce and fertility.

This human tenancy is patiently and insistently regulated by
the Divine will. Islam is strongly 'directional', in that its 'pillars
of religion' and understanding of revelation mean a concerted
and habituated guidance of the human order. Reciting the Qur'ān
gives what we might well call an appropriated currency to the
Divine words themselves. By memory the believer takes into his
mind the text of the Divine mind: by repetition he publicizes
it in a sort of exchange of incorporated attention among the
kindred of faith and as a witness to the outsider. The duties of
the faith corroborate both the solidarity of community and the

habituation of conformity. Together they give powerful impulse and controlling sanction to the fulfilment of religion. Each of them can be interpreted as a rule of relationship to the material bases of life—body, community, property, sustenance and wealth. The *Shahādah*, or witness, makes each Muslim a neighbour in God. 'Performing the prayer'—the Quranic formula for *Ṣalāt*—means a sacramental awareness of the body, a hallowing of the physical existence by its rhythmic, daily, recruitment for the postures of prayer. 'Bring the alms'—an injunction frequently linked with that to prayer—obligates the faithful to a communal responsibility with property and intends for ownership a social conscience. *Ramaḍān*, as the month of fast, imposes a discipline of bodily abstinence as a token of the constant priority of the Divine will, however arduous or seemingly arbitrary, over the clamour and the pressure of personal appetite. Pilgrimage, as its most repeated cry avows, means a self-presentation before God at the rendezvous of Muslim revelation with its earthly instrument: *Labbaika:* 'Here I am before Thee, for Thee', as its double emphatic may be translated. Each of the five duties have wider and more specific meanings than these. But in concert they fashion the temper of Islamic life within the order of the world, and do so with the sustained resources of religious authority. There is powerfully within them a whole philosophy of the relation of man to environment. Muslims would say that they are the Islamic summary of the human privilege in symbol and practice.

But undergirding their feasibility and ensuring their authority is always the necessary context of the Islamic state. The logic of Muḥammad's own sense of the necessity of power in the genesis of Islam enters definitively into its whole history. It is, however, most surely explored in the original expression which the Qur'ān presents, and that, not primarily in the realm of theory but in the growing concreteness of the Prophet's own career. It was this, undoubtedly, which gave to the term *khalīfah* the exclusively political meaning which, as we have seen, it quite noticeably lacked in the first usage. Once Muḥammad's active, and successful, policy of power had inaugurated the ruling precedent, it was inevitable that its perpetuation should be held to be legitimatized by the concept of succession and that the original description of man's tenure under God should have been taken over to denote such rulership.

The point of departure is the fact of opposition. There is no need to review here the familiar story of Muḥammad's steady encounter with hostility, of the vested interests in Mecca which his crusade against idolatry aroused and the courage and tenacity with which he had to sustain his mission through the arduous years before the Hijrah. That event was a pivotal decision, enabling nascent Islam to break out of the impasse in which Meccan obduracy had contained it and to establish in an alternative centre the possibility, and then the robust actuality, of state or city resources for its vindication. By dint of the Medinan consolidation, Muḥammad was able to bring Mecca into his authority within eight years of his departure from it as an apparently frustrated fugitive. There are few more effective or decisive transformations in all history. The finality of Muḥammad's success, set within the logic of his earlier years of unremitting but largely unrewarded fidelity in preaching, wrote its lesson abidingly into the texture of Islamic thought and feeling.

The circumstances within Medina, in the wake of his advent, necessitated the sturdy implementation of the philosophy of power. For once at large from Mecca the opposition there assumed that their stake in his suppression had intensified. Reciprocally Muḥammad needed to anticipate and counter the widened enmity and for this purpose to consolidate his initially tenuous hold upon the Medinan population. The urgency of either objective on the Prophet's side only sharpened the problem of leadership and loyalty. For with the crucial odds ahead, Muḥammad could ill afford subversion or disaffected followers. The triumphantly conclusive outcome to the conflict should not obscure the vital factors of jeopardy and anxiety through which it passed.

It is in this context that the historian has to set the Quranic approbation of defensive watchfulness, its acceptance of the necessity of force and its insistence that extinction is a worse calamity than war. This mind is well summarized, for example, in a passage of principle in Surah 22. 38-40:

Leave is given to those who fight because they are wronged. God is indeed able to bring them to victory; expelled as they were from their dwellings without right for the reason only that they confess God as their Lord. Had not God driven back the people, some by dint of others, cloisters and churches, houses of prayer and mosques wherein the name of God is oft remembered would have been destroyed. Assuredly God comes to the aid of those who come to His. For God is truly all powerful and all strong.

The immediate situation of the Muslim emigrants is here linked with the wider issue of general religious survival, and it is this which lends a special interest to the ruling as a whole. The very continuity of prayer and true worship is said to hinge upon effective counter action to defeat the enemy. Jewish and Christian history would need to claim some exemption from this inclusion. What is significant is that Islam, in this context, assumes no monopoly of necessary retaliation, but, on the contrary, pre-supposes that the external interests of other faiths have rightly turned on it.

'*Fitnah*', then, or subversion, 'is a worse evil than war', as 2. 217 observes. To take the full measure of this decision, it is important to sense an ever present dimension in the Qur'ān, after the Hijrah, namely the fear of insincerity. Muḥammad's vigorous policy of active readiness for combat naturally required a vigilance alert to possible subterfuge or treachery. Yet the very sanctions of power tend to breed precisely such attitudes wherever there is a will to enmity, and they do so the more desperately the greater their external success. Given unresolved contention, or irreducible antipathy, there is likely to be a more sinister quality of con-spiracy against the successful cause, and thus a sort of descending spiral of antagonism and hypocrisy, accentuating each other. There are numerous tokens of this in the Qur'ān, and what is even more significant, an initial sense of its futility.

In the early stages of Muḥammad's mission until the move to Medina, there are notable iterations of the principle that the Prophet's only task is proclamation. Thus Surah 42. 47: 'Giving the message (*al-balāgh*) is your only responsibility', and in 13. 40: 'Your part is simply the giving of the word, Ours (God speaking) is the reckoning'. Surah 10. 100 asks, notably: 'Do you think you can pressure men into becoming believers?' while earlier in the same chapter (10. 46) Muḥammad is confronted in the text with the possibility that he might even die without seeing any fruition of his labour. Again in 10. 104, the warning occurs in a general summary of Islam in Muḥammad's preaching: 'If God visits thee with affliction, none can remove it but He'. This is not, of course, to preclude the later principle that God acts through His people's vigour. But it does hold in its primary relevance an implication of patient trust alone. The parallel between Muḥammad's struggle with obduracy and that of the early patriarchs with their contemporaries, is, of course, a basic fact of Quranic exegesis. All the more notable then the passage in Surah 11 in which Noah labours to win his hostile people. After the council of leaders had protested that Noah had no standing and was followed only by the lowest in the community—a clear echo, it would seem, of the Meccan situation and Quraishī disdain—Noah takes his stand on the authentic revelation given to him and asks: 'If ... it is hidden from you in your blindness, can we (shall we) compel you to accept it against your will?' He disclaims an interest in personal profit and refuses to abandon or disperse the local disciples he has. The steady, humble, patient demeanour of Noah in a context so evidently analogous to the Prophet's adversities makes the posture of a wholly spiritual, even diffident, appeal a significant measure of a vital issue (Surah 11. 27–31).

Three other passages concerned with prophetic precedent and communal antipathy repeat the sole and central duty of faithful utterance: 'Ours is only to deliver the plain truth' (Surah 24. 53; 29. 17 and 36. 16).

It is just the intensity of this encounter which ripens into the decision of which the Hijrah is the crisis and the turning point.

How is prophetic mission related to human rejection? How is Divine vocation to be understood in confrontation with human non-acceptance? What is genuine prophethood to do about irreducible and prolonged defiance of its word? How is the prophetic instrument to see the duty of fidelity to prophetic cause, in the light of the steady, even sharpening, refusal of it? Has loyalty in word finally to pass into vigour of action? Does the message incorporate and validate whatever is needful to its visible and external prosperity and vindication? In a word, must the prophet become the ruler, if he is to achieve the service? Does the inner consistency of revelation require and demand the state? Is religion of necessity political?

To these final questions the answer of Islam is an unhesitating Yes. But it was not immediately so given. There were indeed thirteen years of hesitancy, from the inception of Muḥammad's preaching to his departure from Mecca. These years are the historian's measure of the inward crisis, and the Qur'ān, as we have too briefly seen, reflects how elemental the option was. Some argue that the logic was always there, that what we have in fact is not hesitancy but delay, that Muḥammad's ultimate policy was always implicit. In that event the Hijrah is only a circumstance releasing the occasion, not a purpose in its germination. If we take that view, however, we must reckon with the precedents and directions of the Qur'ān itself in the contrary sense. The option of unrequited patience, of unprovoked ministry, of persistent abiding in the word alone, is one which both patriarchal precedent and Muḥammad's own experience acknowledge.

The political development in original Islam emerges, then, as a definitive thing, 'a consummation devoutly desired', a prescription for religious existence in perpetuity. The Qur'ān is forthright and luminous in its factual and theological reflection of the consequences. Once the active policy of the Medinan period gets under way, we are at once aware, in reading the Qur'ān, of the necessary atmosphere of urgency, of consolidation, of suspicion and of vigilance. There is no need to retell the familiar story of the Prophet's external successes in the campaign against Mecca, nor the careful strategy of his dispositions. By political and material criteria it was an eminently successful and finally magnanimous achievement and a model of vigorous and resourceful leadership. Given the validity of the basic decision, it is also religiously effective. Yet there is no mistaking, with the Qur'ān, the sense of the spiritual price. Once a sanction of prudence is given to allegiance by dint of action, or threat of action, against those who do not believe or are said to conspire, there arises the immediate risk of purely time-serving, or even treacherous, adherence. Force here tends to frustrate its ends precisely by the effects of its means. If one makes it dangerous not to conform, one invites conformists for that reason alone. Sensing the peril of this, one is bound further to suspect and question all such confession of loyalty. Distrust feeds on itself. Reciprocated from the other side, such suspicions only accentuate hypocrisy and provoke the suspects to a more successful disguise of their dubious attitudes, requiring a further countering distrust.

That this descending spiral of suspicion is no idle theory of the situation but a desolating fact is plain from the Qur'ān. It may be focused in the concept of *nifāq*, or hypocrisy. There are numerous passages within the Medinan period, relating to these dissemblers, the *munāfiqūn*. With the convenient non-capitalizing of Arabic initial letters, it is impossible to tell whether they were an actual political party or merely a doubtful element, whether they were moral reprobates or political conspirators. But whether 'hypocrites' or 'Hypocrites' they were certainly a constant menace to the security and prosperity of Muḥammad's cause in circumstances which allowed endless opportunity for dissimulation, plotting, tribal intriguing and sheer human cunning.

Given an implacable intention on their part it is clear that the changed circumstances of Muḥammad's mission provided them paradoxically, with both an incentive and a strategy. As a struggling and hard-pressed minority in Mecca, Muḥammad's early mission was an attractive allegiance for none but the heroic and the sincere. In its Medinan establishment it became at once a prey to conspiratorial insincerity and a magnet for calculating reactions, whether opportunist or malicious. This was the risk it took for its political salvation. It set a situation in which it was tempting for the neutral or the unconvinced to temporize, feigning greater enthusiasm than they felt or professing a firmer commitment than they meant to corroborate if odds changed or pressures eased.

When occasions, like the Battle of Uḥud, brought out clear signs of this less than tenacious adherence, Muḥammad's logic admitted of taking no risks and relaxing no vigilance. Subterfuge was thus the more liable to grow. Surah 63 is particularly concerned with the *munāfiqūn* and has their name for its title. It likens them to 'propped-up timbers', and warns the Prophet against their plausibility, indicating their 'faith' as phoney and their thoughts as treacherous. Elsewhere their influence is seen in unwillingness to join the issues in battle, and in an artful diversion of resolve and discipline. Their vacillations, according to Surah 33, imperilled the Muslim cause in the Battle of the Ditch. There is no need to doubt that in the tangled rivalries and ambitions of the Meccan and Medinan confrontation, and of the Muslim and not-yet Muslim elements within Medina, the machinations of the hypocrites were of crucial sort.

The question, therefore, is not the political validity of the measures by which they were countered and mastered. It is the religious problem implicit in their relation to Muḥammad and the ground on which it turns. The danger is that inner evil becomes identified with external enmity, and that, contrariwise, outward victory becomes synonymous with truth. Wrong is defeated rather than redeemed. It is perhaps significant that with a few exceptions, *nifāq* is not treated in the Qur'ān as a spiritual malady, precisely because its political menace is all engrossing. There is a cryptic expression from time to time associated with these enemies, namely, 'those in whose hearts there is sickness' (cf. Surah 8. 48; 33. 12; 33. 60 and 47. 31). The commentator Al-Baiḍāwī understands this as 'weakness of faith', or 'impiety', and Al-Rāzī associates it with sexual excesses. An Aḥmadiyyah writer goes so far as to relate it to the 'displeasure' (sick-at-heart-ness) with which his detractors regarded his arrival in Medina. It is, thus, the political aspects, the qualities politically culpable, such as vacillation, lip-service and intrigue, that are taken to explain the phrase, which in Biblical categories (cf. Jer. xvii. 9) might well have received a more compassionately moral emphasis. Is it perhaps that the political criteria tend to preclude the deeper analyses of human perversity, precisely because of a pre-occupation with their political anathema?

It is in this way that the Qur'ān provides a most pointed study of the spiritual consequences of giving the sanction of political power to religious belief and community. The lessons recur throughout the history of Islam and have frequent parallel in the political occasions of Judaism and Christendom. For both other faiths have from time to time, though not in essence, pursued an Islamic mind. In his dual role as both supremely a figure of religious affirmation and an architect of religio-political establishment, Muḥammad exemplifies the expression, as power, of the human privilege. Islam is thus the focus politically, no less than Jewry is ethnically, of a crucial interpretation of what it is to be human on behalf of God. The state, with Islam, as people with Jewry, is the crux of our role under God. Where we see the political expression of faith so confidently is where also we learn its deepest tensions.

There is, in Surah 49. 13 and following, an interesting passage in which Muḥammad distinguishes between faith in the heart and allegiance on the lips. It concerns a group of bedouin, probably at a time late in the life of the Prophet, who brought their fealty, saying: 'We believe'. He is directed to check their words, substituting for 'We believe' the verb 'We surrender', with the comment, 'Faith has not yet entered your hearts'. It would be risky to build too much on this isolated passage, though the distinction, if not the contrast, between 'faith' and 'submission' is frequent in the Qur'ān. But in its implication, it seems to establish that there is a kind of (political or politic) accession which does not amount to genuine faith. This may be through ignorance, ill-tuition, uncouthness, or lack of opportunity, rather than deliberate insincerity. Yet, however interpreted, the distinction certainly argues, as vitally necessary, a progression beyond sub-mission, to belief, beyond a politically acceptable allegiance to a religiously authentic heart. It is just both the fact and the necessity of this distinction which the logic emerging from the case of the *munāfiqūn* is concerned to enforce.

We join these two aspects together when we ponder the steady Quranic juncture between God and Muḥammad in the character-ization of the fully Muslim allegiance. The right relation to both is in the due recognition of each. The earthly becomes, in a re-markable way considering Muḥammad's insistent human quality, the touchstone of the heavenly. It is a measure of the political shape of religion in Islam that obedience to God and His messenger are repeatedly conjoined. Thus Surah 5. 56: 'Your loyalty is to God and his apostle', and 5. 93: 'Obey God and obey the apostle'. The former verse even uses the words: *ḥizbullāh* 'the party of God', adding that they are the victorious ones. *Ḥizb* is normally used of a political group. There is in 8. 45 a hint of the ever present demand of politics for solidarity: 'Obey God and obey the messenger and dispute not one with another lest you falter and your power departs'. There are times, legitimately, when a political cause cannot afford the luxury of interior debate or a divided mind. But is it not hazardous to link this necessary cohesion of effective partisanship with the Divine will? Is there not a fundamental necessity in Islam itself of a reservation of the supreme obligation from the requirements of any empirical agency seeking to serve it? For only so can the relativity of politics itself be ensured, and the ultimate antipathy to idolatry be achieved in its own instruments. Are we then here facing a sort of Muslim tension with Islam? It cannot be that insincerity matters only when it takes the form of conspiracy, or that allegiance suffices when it is outwardly docile and accommodating. The peril of identifying the one obedience with the other lies in the temptation to apply purely practical criteria to religious quality and to confuse the latter with effective discipline, a con-clusion which the Qur'ān itself would deplore.

This same theme sharpens if we move to the issues of apostasy. Much unhappy charge and counter-charge needs to be abjured when discussion turns to this topic and a resolute effort made to deal with it in cold detachment and objective, even academic, temper. All communities are naturally tenacious of their adherents and none are exempt from the temptations, or lacking in the art, of forced distraint. There is nothing unique about Islamic instincts at this point. It is rather their peculiarly vigorous pattern of deployment which deserves consideration within the whole setting.

For all the political urgencies we have just studied in the genesis of Medinan Islam, the Qur'ān nowhere specifically empowers or enjoins the community to slay its apostates. The law of apostasy, like so much else in historical Islam, cannot claim indubitable Quranic injunction. The passages, which are for the most part post-Hijrah, may be reviewed as follows. Surah 16. 106 tells of 'the anger of God and a painful punishment' for those, who, having believed, turn away from belief, except under compulsion. What the requital is, however, or whether men should inflict it, is not here stated, though the defection bereaves the perpetrator of all human sympathy or succour. Surah 4. 137, in line with what has been noted above about dubious loyalty, deals with intermittent belief and disbelief, and withdraws all forgiveness or guidance from those who settle into a stubborn posture of denial. Surah 3. 86 and following verses declare the curse of God upon all who abandon belief for disbelief, and, indeed, the curse also of angels and of men. 'Their chastisement shall not be lightened and there is for them no respite from torment.' It adds, though, that God forgives the repentant—a point which, it might be argued, precludes a capital punishment, inasmuch as death forestalls all repentance. Those who die unbelieving could not ransom themselves with a whole earth full of gold.

Explicitly, then, the idea that death must be the penalty of apostasy is not Quranic. Nevertheless, the identity of faith with state discipline is as imperative for Islamic criteria, as the identity of faith with blood membership is for Hebraic. As traditionally conceived, there is a sort of religious tribalism about each. The freedom of accession into Islam means an open community but only in one direction. The related concept of tolerated minorities, or *dhimmis*, within Muslim territory, embodies and assumes the doctrine that religious faith is a matter of birth. The distinct religious adherence, allowed if one is born into it, is at the same time a distinction of a political nature. Conversely the Islamic allegiance is constituted, not in conviction alone, but in legal status of a binding kind.

Contemporary pressures have, of course, modified in practice these classic facts of *Dār al-Islām*. There has been widespread secularization of law. But there remains in powerful, emotional and spiritual 'substance', this definitive concept of state-expression as integral to the existence of a valid Islam. The concurrence in nationalism of the urge to political independence and of the contemporary fulfilment of Islam tends strongly to corroborate the historic assumption of the role of the state in Islamic being.[1] It is fair to say that the primacy of the political in Islamic renewal in the last half-century has been in modern terms the translation of the formative assumptions of the first quarter-century of its origins. No doubt, on the negative side, the halting and ousting of western, imperial authority has required this vigorous assertion of a political consciousness. But this should not obscure the deep, positive character within it. The concern for statehood reproduces in the current scene the sturdy reliance of Islam's beginnings on the central efficacy, within religion, of the political dimension.

Nowhere is the theme of religious power so categorically stated as by Islam and that in itself has the merit of excluding evasive ambiguity. Other faiths, of contrasted temper in their origins, have brought it the frequent tribute of imitation. It seems no more, and no less, than the honest translation of ultimate conviction into active and effective being. What, in the end, can be the value of an unrealized ideal or of an inoperative intent? Power, sooner or later, and probably sooner, is inescapable. It may represent temptations

[1] Some effort to illustrate and review this theme will be found in the writer's *Counsels in Contemporary Islam*, Edinburgh, 1965.

inimical to religious integrity and moral truth. But if it is imagined that for the sake of these risks power itself must be foregone, then there are different perils and no means to counter them. There is, finally, in the human situation no vacuum into which we can fit the luxury of our Gethsemanes. There are only the canons of vigour and of struggle and of power. Even the wistful poetry with which we greet the pathos of our sufferers-for-truth is a kind of fallacy of compensation to relieve the failure of their ends. Effectiveness, in the end, must be the criterion even of compassion. The logic of life is power and the theme of religion is submission. The marriage of these is power-submission, and this is Islam. One does not truly submit unless one prevails. For victory is with God.

This is, so to speak, the transcendental dimension of Islam. It can certainly be reinforced, even if it is not historically derived, from factors in Muḥammad's immediate setting.[1] Whereas Christianity emerged in the context of a mighty empire, strongly in possession, Islam grew in the midst of tribal pluralism in chronic need of unity and order. There had been, antecedently to Muḥammad, eager efforts after consolidation.[2] It is probable that the *Ḥanīfs*, prior to the rise of Islam, had realized the relation of tribal deities to tribal divisions and had sought, without the thorough success which attended Muḥammad, a political answer to the confusions of idolatry. Obscurities necessarily attach to such conjecture, but there can be no doubt that there were earlier movements towards Arab unity and that they had faltered in the face of local religious loyalties they had been unable to surmount. When Muḥammad's prophethood and statesmanship achieved the factors necessary to such mastering of the obstacles, it was natural that his leadership should take political form.

The opposition itself was in considerable measure also political. The preaching of Muḥammad could hardly have remained, in a

---

[1] The next Chapter, *inter alia*, will deal with the suggestion made in some quarters that original Christianity was not political, only because conditions deterred it from so being. The only concern of the present argument is with circumstances in the genesis of Islam and not with comparison.

[2] Cf. Alfred Guillaume, *Islam*, London, 1954, Ch. 1.

largely illiterate and traditional society, a mere spiritual option of opinion and adherence. Its central emphases ran directly contrary to the plain and vested interests of the Meccan hegemony. It could not have been supposed, prior to the so called return pilgrimage after the post-Hijrah warfare, that pilgrimage as an institution could survive the general acceptance of the Prophet's witness. For idolatry had hitherto been the ground and sanction of pilgrimage and Muḥammad's message dethroned all gods and denounced all *shirk*, or pluralized worship. On the continuation of pilgrimage turned the general prestige and much of the commercial prosperity of Mecca. In point of fact, of course, Islam made of Meccan pilgrimage, minus the idols, a far more central and enriching thing. But the Quraish in Mecca could not have known this in advance. Their resistance, therefore, to Muḥammad in its political quality argued a no less insistent political character in his enterprise against the religious sources of their animosity and on behalf of his doctrines of faith. Iconoclasm, in that situation, if not in every situation, is essentially political, since one cannot otherwise be forcible. The competition of belief was by its nature an argument in power. There is little evidence, in Mecca at any rate, of dogged devotion to the idols. The capitulation was much more an acquiescence in the logic of facts, or at least a belief that if the idols had been unable to defend themselves and their shrine dwellers, there remained no ground for their defence.

It is difficult then to visualize in the setting of original Islam a purely spiritual or doctrinal encounter with its world. There was no strong authority for it to invoke in protection. The death of Abū Ṭālib, the Prophet's uncle, removed the only such shelter he enjoyed and then only in severely personal terms. The cover which some Muslims found in Ethiopia was clearly no abiding solution for their Arabian cause. When there was persecution, grievous as it was, it came from an establishment, forceful enough in its malevolence, yet not overwhelmingly dominant to the point of forestalling every thought of viable resistance. We put the point differently if we say that there could conceivably have been no Hijrah from the Roman Empire had Islam originated in the markets of Rome or Antioch. There was no Yathrib anywhere in the Roman realm ready to become by dint of opportunist skill 'the city of the Prophet'.

To reflect on these historical and local factors is to make the pragmatic case for Islam as it was and in concrete terms to justify its philosophy of power. The theological case, as Islam sees it, simply derives from, and reinforces, the pragmatic. Only in states do men truly possess and achieve their destiny.

The state from the Islamic viewpoint is the means whereby the Islamic concepts of life are realized in a definite human organization. The ultimate reality, according to the Qur'ān, is spiritual but the life of the state consists in its temporal activity. The Spirit finds its opportunities in the natural, the material, the secular.[1]

The state's being the form of the Islamic spirit turns, as a doctrine, upon Muslim understanding of history. Just as, for the Hebrew tradition, Hebraic existence bears, as it were, a Divine *imprimatur* as the true humanity,[2] so in Muslim conviction, Islamic authority carries a unique validation as a Divine establishment of truth. History is seen as vindicating the right and distinctively so in what has to do with Islam. There is almost here a kind of empirical 'election', not of course racial, but, as it were, factual.

The cause of history itself is a moral agency through which the morally superior elements rise to the top, while those who are morally inferior sink to the bottom . . . That virtuous living, which is the outcome of a healthy religious faith, must inevitably lead to success and the possession of political power, has been repeatedly stressed in the Qur'ān.[3]

Surah 24. 55 is cited in this connection with its assurance of secure and sustained hegemony, together with Surah 21. 105 where the Qur'ān in one of its very rare occasions quotes directly from the Bible, that is Ps. xxxvii. 29. 'As for the earth, it shall be the inheritance of my righteous servants.' The pledge here is taken in

---

[1] H. Z. Nuseibeh, *The Ideas of Arab Nationalism*, Ithaca, N.Y., 1956, p. 23.

[2] The thought which may underlie the Biblical phrase 'son of man'. See M. D. Hooker, *The Son of Man in Mark*, London, 1967.

[3] Mazheruddin Siddiqi, *The Quranic Concept of History*, Karachi, 1965, pp. 7–8.

a quite literal sense, as giving history a moral discrimination that works towards the prosperity of believers, who may, in turn, see in their external power the seal of the Divine favour.

The simplicity of this confidence is attractive and the first generations of Islam had reason to hold it unsuspectingly. Though, significantly, it would hardly fit Islam itself in the most creative period of its pre-Hijrah adversity, it is a perpetuation, in theological consistency, of the post-Hijrah success. Islam, as Nuseibeh points out, never had to revise for centuries its conviction of state authenticity[1] or emerge, like Christianity, from a period of persecuted subjection into a reversing adaptation to power. It never had, that is, a Constantine effectuating a revolution in its fortunes for ever beset by the misgivings bequeathed by its origins in docility and political innocence. From the outset of its Constantinian Muḥammad, it enjoyed the steady asset of sophisticated power.

Or perhaps it is the very sophistication of Islam in this context that should be described as 'innocent'. For it is clear, Quranically, that the definitive inaugural history is understood and accepted as for all time the confirmation of this view of righteous power. It is a simplification seemingly untrammelled by any tragic perspective or deterred by any adverse experience. And it is unsuspecting in its self-approval. It seems, by criteria other than its own, a quite remarkable unawareness of dimensions of guilt and pathos, in itself and others—dimensions that are normally central to the sense of history. Subsequent experiences, not least in modern times, have gone far to modify this feature of Muslim mentality, not least the recent era of imperial mastery from the west, during which the course of Islamic history seemed to the faithful to have gone grievously awry[2] and there was for every Muslim the

---

[1] In the sense, here, of the basic legitimacy of the political on behalf of the religious. There were of course numerous issues, in the Ummayyad period and after, of misgiving about particular rulers, and many searching thoughts among the *Khawārij* and others on the right of non-obedience.

[2] Cf. W. C. Smith, *Islam in Modern History*, Princeton, 1955, p. 41: 'The fundamental malaise of modern Islam is a sense that something has gone wrong with Islamic history . . . the fundamental problem . . . is how to rehabilitate that history'.

taxing question of whether, under such foreign domination, *Dār al-Islām*, the true 'household', really existed. Could it be said to be intact only by virtue of piety and the *Shahādah* and the works of devotion; or did it necessitate rule of Muslims by Muslims?[1] Other factors in these same times, refugeedom, war and partition, as well as the age-long wretchednesses of poverty and hunger, have given to the mystery of suffering a more crucial place in the Muslim dialogue of faith with life. Throughout, too, and not to be forgotten in any disquisition on the political, runs the wealth of Sūfī mysticism, its sensitivities lying well beneath the surface of historical optimism.

Yet the theology of politics in Islam only slowly and reluctantly revises its familiar confidence about a traditional equation of power and truth. The saving grace of that tradition lies in its corollary that the state is instrumental. In the genesis of faith prophecy is prior. Muḥammad is first preacher. What follows the Hijrah is for the sake of what precedes it. Statehood is sought imperatively because faith is in the field affirmatively. That symbol of precedence dominates all theory and the original in-strumentality of the state always judges its activity. The authority of rulers is only established by God in order to ensure the applica-tion of the sacred law. Government is the means to the *Sharīʿah*. All sovereignty is God's, and thus its earthly exercise must always be tributary and, in the last resort, accountable. The political has no ultimacy of its own. The state is right only as an organ of metaphysical obligation. We need not here explore the various appeals to this principle as requiring or allowing a conditional allegiance from the subject. It was invoked, for example, by Maulānā Āzād within Indian Islam in the nineteen forties, to fortify the case against partition on the ground that even an Islamic state in the terms a Pakistan partition case demanded would not *ipso facto* be right or deserve obedience.[2] It was claimed,

---

[1] The most convenient nineteenth-century example of this theme would be the issue drawn between Aḥmad Khān and his critics in the attempt to re-invigorate Indian Islam after 1857. See *Counsels, op. cit.*, Ch. 2.

[2] See Mahadev Desai, *Mawlānā Abū-l-Kalām Āzād*, London, 1941, pp. 79, 80.

contrariwise, by Pakistan advocacy, as making separate Islamic statehood a condition of a proper assent by Muslims to government at all. In the subsequent history of Pakistan the precise shape and sufficient guarantees of true Islamicity in the state have been strenuously argued and variously interpreted.

These divergencies concern us here only within the central notion of God and state. For there is the gist of the Islamic version of the human privilege as being religiously grounded and politically achieved. How, in conclusion, does its own intention find it? In attempting an answer it is clear that we are also assessing many other, if less forthright, historical occasions outside Islam of reliance on the same belief. The dilemma which we find emerging brings us close to problems that are especially acute in the current scene.

In a narrative passage describing Muḥammad's initial experience as a prophet, in Surah 53, Gabriel is figured approaching from the horizon to within 'two bows' length or nearer' (53. 9). One recent commentator takes the verse metaphorically to mean 'two bows served by one string',[1] and links this meaning with the intimate unity between God's will and Muḥammad's mission, as a 'spiritual fusion', through which submission and direction become one. Ideally stated, and therefore supremely evaluated, this is the Islamic intention, the identity of the willing and the doing.

So understood, the inward dilemma appears. Can the sacred be thus entrusted, or the custody be so total? Are there not necessary reservations, so to speak, in the Divine purpose, without which the agency itself loses true subordination? Does this close mutuality between truth and power, between God and the state, propose an impossibly sanguine juncture between the ultimate and the relative, the eternal and the pragmatic, the will of heaven and the competence of men? Is it a misreading, by optimism, of the privilege of man? And, thereby, in turn, a compromise of the majesty of God?

These questions are perhaps abstrusely put. In sharper terms,

[1] Zafrullah Khan, *Islam*, New York, 1962, p. 26.

we are confronted, on reflection here, by the partiality of the political order. As we have already noted in pondering the *munāfiqūn* and the proneness of power to provoke insincerity, there is always a sense in which the victories of force forfeit by their very terms the full dimensions of truth. 'The will to power', as has been noted, 'is a servile will', insofar as it foreshortens the tasks of truth. Ultimate victories are never violent. There is a deep over-simplification in a political salvation. For it is in danger all the time of exempting its own agency from the judgement of the sovereignty it serves—a fatal flaw already recognized in Jewish ethnicism. It tends to identify the good with its success, and the right with its cause. And insofar as it stays within the political and the forceful, it leaves reaches of human evil unrecognized and unrelieved.

The logic of this realization is not to disown or discredit or dismiss the political altogether. On the contrary, as Islam so well exemplifies, it has duties and achieves ends which are positive and valid and which an idle piety could never satisfy. Yet it is wise to see them as also relative. We need not be as severe as the dictum which alleges that all the state can do is to hinder the hindrances to the good.[1] For there is, as Islam has confidently shown, a spiritual dimension to statehood which makes it much more than a mere policing of humanity. Yet human autonomy has a way of revenging itself on forcible submissions. If we will not risk apostates, we cannot hold free men. Truth is itself untruthful if it makes scepticism a crime and doubt a treachery. Power can keep the ring as it were for forces of justice and righteousness, both from within itself and from beyond itself, which otherwise might lack a present opportunity. Power must be ever aware that there are also forces, not only from outside itself, but necessarily *against itself*, which cannot be gainsaid and which will not be suborned. For their business may disqualify and repudiate the state itself. It is these considerations which call in question the over ready marriage of the Islamic service of God with the agency of political reliance.

[1] Bernard Bosanquet, *Philosophical Theory of the State*, London, 1899, p. 191.

These considerations, precisely, are those which the contemporary world puts in sharper focus than any other time. Arising from the secular forces which must be seen, as we have argued, to be squarely within the caliphate of man, and not, therefore, to be excluded or deprived, there is an increasing assertion of human autonomies and these present a steadily intensifying challenge to any attempt to comprehend human existence within any framework of Divine relation, least of all one which establishes itself by assertive identity with the transcendent and enforces itself by political expression. It is for this reason that the whole traditional concept of *Dār al-Islām*, 'the household of the faith', is in radical question, either as feasibility or fact. The secularizing of society, of law, of economy, of education, makes it ever harder to define and more dubious still to actualize. Politically also the trend, even in homogeneously Muslim communities, is strongly towards the secularizing of the state, and where societies are pluralist and heterogeneous the process is wellnigh imperative. In these circumstances, Islam becomes of necessity more and more a religion in the sense which, classically, Muslims would regard as partial and invalid, namely as being a pattern of worship, a mission of hallowing, a life of the spirit, without benefit of state monopoly and even without political sanction.

Herein, of course, lies a drastic revolution, variously registered and sustained in different parts of the Islamic world. There is no place here to record its sequences or gauge its future. But it is fair to observe, given the characteristic politico-religious pattern of Islam we have reviewed, that there is no contemporary faith more radically involved in the issue of secularity. For there is no faith that has so ambitiously or so programmatically related the human order and the Divine will. The tradition of Islam, unlike the other monotheisms, has not in general approved a relative contention for social righteousness that conceded an intractability in the human situation, while striving for an inward conversion of human nature that both respected and revolutionized the wayward will. Rather its whole instinct was to assume and enjoin a viable tractability, short of regeneration and made feasible by state action. Any other posture its theology regarded as bemeaning the force of the Divine will and making an improperly pessimistic, or even defamatory, reading of humanity. In a day, therefore, when the religious reference of human affairs is more and more challenged by the secular possession of the world and the spiritual loss of the self, Islam has the merit, which is also the burden, of exemplifying in bold and plain terms the dilemma of the religious world-view. Can there be the apostle of God other than with the rule of God? Or is there, about the human situation as religion learns and serves it, at once a larger crisis and a deeper tragedy?

VI

Grace and Sonship:
The Crisis of Christian Humanity

'LIFE is so short, and so ridiculous and irrational (from a certain point of view) that one knows not what to make of it, unless, well ... finish the sentence for yourself.'[1] So Herman Melville in one of his letters. His own immediate solution in such moods was to take ship, where the soul might 'keep the open independence of her sea'.[2] But that was a device which later he was denied. And, in any event, it only gave the mystery a wider, deeper reach, as *Moby Dick* reveals.

How, essentially, does Christian faith conclude the sentence? What is the essential Christian understanding of the human meaning? How is it to be identified in the wealth of Christian tradition and the complexities of Christian history? Do we begin and end with the Sermon on the Mount? How does the Cross and the Resurrection beyond it bear upon our answer? Is Paul the true mentor or the misleader? What of the gibe that there was only one Christian and He was a Jew? Is it to Nazareth, or Jerusalem, or Antioch, or Rome we must go to learn?

Let it rather be, in this context, to Mecca and Judea. The hope here is to study the Christian humanism, as already anticipated in the dimensions of Abraham, by way of the contrast with the themes of Judaism and Islam which we have now reviewed. Since the obligation of our whole study is comparative, this proceeding has more than the asset of novelty. It has illuminating possibilities to which it may give sharp focus and a clearer perspective than might be attained by a more general approach. While the three faiths depend for their diversities upon the strong ties of identity that bind them, it is by the former that they best instruct the enquirer into their mind and ethos.

[1] *Letters of Herman Melville*, New Haven, 1960, p. 260.
[2] *Moby Dick*, New York, 1944 ed., p. 133.

The point of departure, then, is the Jewish sense of destiny and the Islamic sense of power, each as we saw taken instrumentally to the Divine will and seen as embodying the ultimate privilege of man. The chosen nation and the Divinely ordered state believe themselves possessed of the true dignity of custodian for God. There is the Jewish 'hallower' or 'sanctifier' of creation, the priestly people on behalf of all, the perpetuation of the Abrahamic seed in full physical reality. And there is the Islamic 'actualizer' of the heavenly will, by the aegis of the Islamic *ummah*, conceived in full political validity, until there is no more place among men for *fitnah*, or unruliness.

Christianity, historically, contrasts clearly and unmistakeably with both of these, though from the same commitment to the Divine sovereignty and the same human dominion. It parts company with the particularism of Israel and it diverges from the power invocation of Islam.[1] Its new covenant by its open character breaks out of the ethnic framework and by its gentle quality abjures and disallows the sanction of force and the persuasions of political authority. The reasons within these decisions lie deep in the ministry of Jesus, in his understanding and achievement of Messiahship as the Church receives it, and in the experience of sonship to God as it derived from the recognition there of the filial obedience, through word and suffering, by which Jesus had 'loved the Father'. These sources, which we must explore, of the openness and gentleness of the Christian Gospel constituted a radical crisis for the Jewish world within which they belonged. In the event, the genesis of the Church, though it was a profoundly Jewish fact both in personnel and concept, left corporate Jewry unpersuaded and unready to allow itself such 'church' fulfilment, unconvinced, that is, that openness of covenant could be universal or that Messiahship could be seen as accomplished. It clung to the communal distinctiveness and the moral feasibility of the law

---

[1] It may seem anachronistic to write in the present tense in these terms before Islam existed. But it will be clear in all that follows that there were deep 'Islamic' issues in the very making of Christianity and it is in no essential way anticipatory to see them side by side. See below.

against the Christian claim that both had been overtaken by the
reality of grace and the equality within it of the peoples of the
larger world. This unwillingness of Jewry to become 'church'
left vexing legacies to the new community and there was a growing tendency to identify 'Christian' with 'Gentile'. But this fact,
and the problems associated with it, should not obscure the underlying quality of Christianity as a critical achieving of all that the
old covenant had inaugurated, and of ongoing Jewry as a decisive
exemption, by its own will, from such a destiny. Only in this way
will it be clear that the Christian account of God and man
involves a revolutionary relation to every other context.

This is certainly so by the Islamic measure. It was agreed, in the
previous Chapter, that the social and political conditions in the
Hijāz in Muḥammad's day could be said to have made inevitable
the political pattern of his mission after the Hijrah. When the
contrast with the unified, disciplined authority of Rome in Jesus'
day is noted, it sometimes becomes the ground for the claim that
the Gospel is 'docile' and politically passive only because any
defiance of the empire would have been foolhardy and doomed
from the beginning. It is necessary to eliminate this notion, as the
evidence overwhelmingly demands we should, if the genuine,
interior quality of decisiveness about Jesus' pattern of ministry is
not to be obscured. It was emphatically *not* because Rome left a
Messiah no other option that Jesus is found in his Gethsemane. It
is well not to underestimate the popular potential of his leadership
and charismatic grace if we are assessing these imponderables.
Had the figure whom the Gospels describe chosen to set himself
at the head of a popular rising, Pilate would certainly have had
much more to do than wash his hands. The feeder of the multi-
tude, the cleanser of the Temple, the healer of the throngs, the
master who, however paradoxically, could accept the acclaim of
Palm Sunday, could readily have kindled a conflagration in Judea
consuming enough to threaten even Rome itself. There were, it
must be remembered, ample precedents for such Messianism.
The Maccabees had not lived in vain. It is a very precarious argument to imagine that the Christhood of Jesus was dictated simply

by Roman imperial majesty denying any other practicable alternative.

It is also a total misreading of the New Testament. There were, plainly, zealots among Jesus' disciples. It could well be that Judas' 'betrayal' was in fact an effort on the part of one of them to precipitate the sort of militant action which they sought, and which Jesus had so tantalizingly failed to take, by the device of confronting him with a final dénouement. If so, his refusal to be precipitated only demonstrates with dramatic force the steady set of his own mind and their utter miscalculation. The presence of those zealots, however, is eloquent of Jesus' concern for the things they mistakenly sought by violence and rebellion, namely redemption in Israel and the freedom of the hearth.[1] But they were balanced, no less eloquently, by the 'publicans and sinners' with whom, aside from the strange unity of Jesus' company, they could not co-exist. For these were the quislings of the time, the anti-patriots who stooped to personal profit out of national dismay. Simon the Zealot and Matthew the publican, side by side in discipleship, witness to a Master who intends no evasion of the real world and no cheap salvation that excludes its castaways. The effort, in what follows, to penetrate the inner core of Jesus' Messianic decision, understood as the working out of his sense of sonship to the Father, leaves at least this writer with no other possible conclusion than that the gentleness of the kingdom of heaven, in his hands, is none other than a free, courageous, steadfast *choice*, sustained against all odds, patient through all misunderstandings, and rooted

[1] S. G. F. Brandon, *Jesus and the Zealots*, Manchester, 1967, purports to show that Jesus was in fact a Zealot or para-Zealot and cites in this cause certain Gospel sayings, including 'cross-bearing', and 'the kingdom of heaven suffering violence'. But it is significant that his theory has to ignore the relevance of the publicans and that he must needs postulate that the Gospels, all of them, are tendentiously adjusted to dissociate the Church from complicity in the Jewish Revolt. The very necessity of such a hypothesis is itself suspicious. There are better explanations of the evidence and deep elements, like the Holy Communion, are given less than justice. It is natural that interpretations of Jesus, his policy and the onus for his death, should remain acutely sensitive areas of study. But we can hardly explain the crux of his Messiahship as a tendentious and *post facto* invention to serve an innocuous church.

in communion with God. It is on this account that it is fitted to be the inclusive sacrament of the Divine way with men and response to it, therefore, the fullest experience of the human privilege. The only point here, in noting the tangled controversies which dispute or otherwise interpret the facts of the history, is to deny their claim to depreciate or qualify this central verdict. Their importance lies, rather, in the entail of that decision in the subsequent character of the Church and in the controversies between the old and the new. It was almost inevitable that issues between Christianity and Jewry should become involved in contention about the circumstances of the death of Jesus and that history itself should become the battle-ground of its own legacies. There is about the central meaning a quality beyond invention and beyond dispute. It is this we must seek and ponder.

'SON OF THE FATHER'

The pattern of Jesus as the Christ, alternate both to Hebrew reliance upon law and covenant people and to Islamic pursuance of the political kingdom as that to which all else is added, emerges within his ministry as a compelling alertness to the capacities of grace and the cost of evil. Humanity is seen there to involve a reach of need and of obligation which are not to be satisfied by external authority, whether of the law or of the state. Hence there is immediate realism both in diagnosis and in hope. Are not the Gospels alive, even at first glance, with just this quality of penetration, of frankness, scattering the clouds of illusion and falsity, fresh as the open-air in which so much of the ministry and the preaching was set? The content of the teaching is in ready contact with the living situations of the time, in contention with its prevailing errors, and in ready alliance with the natural order.

It was to primal simplicities that the teacher recalled his hearers. 'Consider the lilies . . .', 'behold, the fowls of the air . . .'. Nature, with a lively kinship, yielded his parables and kindled his images. 'The word was made flesh' even in this spoken sense, in that the message of trust in nature's God as in a Father was set so sweetly within the processes of farming and harvest, of birds and flowers.

This trustworthiness in the shape of natural events was only one aspect of the sonship to which men were called. 'Your heavenly Father knoweth...', he took to be the assurance within the physical world. The elemental search of man for security and for good was satisfied through the husbandry of the good earth. 'Anxious thought' could, therefore, be excluded. God, as Jesus preached Him, dealt with men as sons by the dependable mysteries in which they were fed, sheltered, renewed and furnished, as the wealth of nature gave them means. The Divine Fatherhood was not a doctrine simply: it was the practice of a reliance, the sense of an everlasting mercy in the things of time and sense, and could be reciprocated as sonship, in glad, confident dependence.

But Jesus, in his teaching, spoke of a realism which penetrated, no less surely, into the other realm of human experience, into the dark shadows of self-will and pride. The veils of self-righteousness he tore apart, with a firm exposure of the evil motives which may lie at the heart of seeming goodness. Men were in need to search their hearts perpetually. For in the motive lay the crux. If convention or convenience alone held in check the evil will, wrong was already there and culpable. Seeming goodness is all too liable to inward evil, since men habitually like to deceive, and be deceived, in their own favour. Hence the sharp anathemas of the Gospels against the religious establishment and the forms of piety. The self-righteous man goes into the temple and his very prayers are a panegyric on himself. There is a vitiating pride that pursues even the holiest forms.

This is what Jesus perceives to be the original sin of men, an evil at the very heart of them, not derived from outward things but pervading from within the motives of the heart, perverting righteousness and undoing merit. It does not mean that they are totally corrupt but that there is no part of them, reason, will, or emotion, beyond the range of its distortion. It is for this cause that the salvation of men can never arise simply from their 'works' since these, by their nature, have themselves to be included in the saving.

From this same dimension sprang another feature of the words of Jesus, one which deeply antagonized his public foes. If 'the common people heard him gladly', it was not simply that the parables were homely and his talk direct. It was because, as they listened, vistas of hope and possibility opened before them which established authority had closed. Matthew, Zaccheus, Mary Magdalene, folk whose failures and lapses had set them beyond the pale of a meritorious ethic, saw new hope for them and their kind in his version of the kingdom of heaven. The prodigal can never return home if the only hope of a welcome lies in never having strayed. The sinner, by the Pharisees' book is, like a fallen runner, out of the race. Or so it seemed, to those who had dropped out of the aristocracy of legal merit. So the teaching of Jesus opened up a new door of hope to the despised of the world. 'Thou hast opened the kingdom of heaven to all believers' was already a truth of his ministry before it became the praise of his passion. It was this offer of an undefeated potential of grace which the Church learned from his words. The whole shocked reaction of legalism is in the words: 'Who is this that forgiveth sins?'

There were, in all this, not a few echoes of the old order, from prophet and psalm and rabbi. There is neither right, nor need, to claim a total originality for the message Jesus proclaimed. What the Christian faith does hold, however, is that there was a co-hesion and an integrity about the truth he ministered, and an enduring efficacy—witness the pervasive recurrence of his 'imitation' in the pages of the Epistles and the whole consensus of the New Testament. By the words of Jesus, as John Wesley phrased it, men 'exchanged the faith of a servant for the faith of a son'. And all because of the deep sonship to the Father, out of which Jesus spoke and by which he was moved, a sonship which he communicated to his listeners, by the sense of the dignity that God's trust in them bestowed and by the endless possibilities of the grace with which He greeted them.

These reflections are in no sense a complete or adequate study of the teaching of Jesus and are not so intended. But, for all their brevity, they serve to preface the origins of the crucifixion. It was just this world where the prodigal returns, the Samaritan binds the wounds, the publican prays in penitence—the world of grace and healing in unlikely places—that risks and incurs the clash with establishment and law. The opposition which finally sought his liquidation arose out of the reaction to his message, and by his loyalty to all that he had said he moved in steady self-consistency into the climax of suffering. If he had not taught as he did, there need have been no impulse to his death. But equally, if he had not embraced that sacrifice his teaching would have been an arch lacking the keystone of its whole integrity. There is a sense in which it is doubtful whether Jesus would have in fact been a historical personality at all, had he not suffered on the Cross. This does not mean that his teaching has survived only because a community was mysteriously created out of his death and passion. What it does mean is that, by death, teaching was sanctioned into perpetuity, in that by the Cross it was most perfectly exemplified and achieved.

It is just here that we come upon the element of decisive choice in the ministry of Jesus. 'The Gospel as Jesus proclaimed it', wrote Harnack somewhere, now long ago, 'has to do with the Father only and not with the Son.' By this, presumably, he meant to give crisp expression to the once popular view that the teaching of Jesus about Divine Fatherhood could be readily and properly separated from the orthodox dogma about his status in sonship to God, the latter being a theological subtlety, far removed from the fresh winds of Galilee and the Sermon on the Mount. But better perspectives have firmly disproved this suggestion. The terms 'Father' and 'Son' are, anyway, reciprocal and cannot be affirmed in any sort of antithesis within one analogy. Jesus' words about the Father spring from his own aliveness as 'Son'. He was not preaching a notion, but an experience. There was a depth of filial awareness, breathing such prayers as: 'Father, thy will . . .', 'Father, into thy hands . . .', 'Father, I thank thee . . .', and the rest.

Christian faith at its wisest has seen this filial converse of Jesus with God as the active spring both of the teaching about God which he commended to his hearers, and of the choices by which he corroborated that message within the context set for him by the situation of his time and vocation. The way in which he understood and accomplished Messiahship is the meaning, in the concrete, of his sonship.[1] The pattern, of course, was wrought out in the midst of deep popular misconceptions and deceptive alternatives and ill-assorted hopes, which the disciples themselves shared. Indeed, ideas of Messiah might be said to be the first situation Messiah had to save. Thus it was that Jesus moved in the midst of ambiguity, where the 'who?' of Messianic identity had to be subdued to the 'how?' of Messianic policy. To be taken for Messiah, but in terms of militancy and strife and political action, would have been to falsify and partialize salvation. To take suffering redemptively and establish it as the true Messianic mystery—this was the supreme task.

To have reckoned, first in spirit and then in action, with this calling is the 'filiality' of Jesus, the meaning in the active of Sonship to the Father. It is the ability to pray: 'The cup which my Father has given me . . .'—the heart to know and to take the Cross as the true mind of the Lord. This is the Son through whom we have the Father. Nor is it a theory of metaphysics: it is rather sweat and blood and Gethsemane and a crown of thorns. Jesus saw it this way because of his openness both to God and men. 'The Son', says a New Testament writer, 'learned obedience . . .' An answer to the human predicament that is only political must needs leave 'remainders' unsatisfied. Its compulsiveness will compromise its qualities and exclude the enemies it has to make along the way. More violent answers expend and alienate them. A meritorious salvation, based on law, has no room for prostitutes and prodigals. It is condemnatory and selective and even with its successes leaves the door open to vitiating prides and prejudice.

Only gentleness and openness in the ways of grace can be said to intend and pursue an answer to the human situation which has no 'remainders' of unredeemed or excluded realms of evil or of

---

[1] As it is also, by definition, the first and active meaning of 'Christology', despite the technical, abstract, ontological monopoly of this term as generally used.

will. But, by the same token, they necessarily suffer. Because they do not resist, or resent, or revenge, they 'take' the whole weight of the wrongness and, so doing, undertake its full retrieval, in a way that force or compulsion, however seemingly efficient, do not. By its uncomplicated directness and simplicity in the cause of truth, a love that suffers incurs the whole antipathy and thereby achieves a whole salvation. Retaliation, or preventive action, somehow 'justify' the original enmity by corroborating its instincts. Only love 'reduces' it to peace. Where resentment breeds defiance, and exclusion indifference or despair, redemption retrieves and reconciles and re-instates. But in these achievements it bears itself the evil it surmounts, and it is this which is inevitably costly and self-expending.

The whole logic of the Gospels turns upon this sense of things in the mind and 'policy' of Jesus as the Christ. And if we ask how he came to see it so, the answer must take us to what classically is defined by calling him 'the Son of the Father'. There is no tautology in this phrase. We are moving in two realms, the actuality of a history and the definition of a theology. The meaning of Christianity is that both are cruciform. What happens in the sharp actuality of Galilee and Jerusalem is read as the expression of the eternal mind. What God is and what the Christ does are held to be two aspects of one reality, two only because in time and beyond time, in history and in truth. Just as, in the Old Testament, the Messianic expectation springs from confidence in the Divine sovereignty, so its New Testament achievement is read as disclosing what, and how, that sovereignty is. The being of God and the doing of the Christ have a mutually descriptive character.

Two elements in this faith about God in Christ must be carefully recollected—the one that the whole is rooted in real events, the other that it belongs integrally with the whole shape of Jesus' teaching. Christian theology has sometimes been tempted to artificialize the transactions of salvation, to see them necessitated, as it were, by *a priori* notions, even subtleties, of a doctrinal kind. Theories of the Incarnation and of atonement have been prone to suggest a sort of deductive abstraction, whereby Jesus suffers to satisfy justice, or to enable pardon, or to 'square' law. But these are, at best, only rational formulations, at worst unhappy distortions, of a free, critical, magnificent, reality of redemptive self-oblation, happening in a living context of representative enmity and undertaking its inclusive transmutation. We can never comprise Gethsemane and Calvary in an academic formula. The encounter they bring to a climax must be known as a cumulative reckoning with a coalition of human evils, ecclesiastical, political, social and individual, which deserve to be seen as a full epitome of the likeness of men. They are 'the sin of the world' in that inclusive sense. Our humanity is qualitatively known where it gathers, round the Cross. The Pilates, the Herods, the Caiaphases, the mobs, the Judases, of that situation, are the mirrors of us all. Nothing here is staged, or artificial, occurring to fit a book or argue a theory. It is a living, spontaneous, damning disclosure of what evil is and does and, therefore, by the same token, of what love must do with it and about it, in its whole integrity. As such, it is not an accident, nor, properly read, a tragedy. It is a transaction in compassion, the 'measure for measure' of God with men.

The antecedents of the event belong in the teaching we have already pondered. Both must be held in one. We must not take a view of Jesus' passion, as for example Schweitzer did, which would relate it to eschatological or other concepts inferior to the actual practice of his ministry. It does not spring from some forlorn attempt to force the hand of heaven in despair over a thwarted purpose otherwise conceived. To think this would be incongruous with the whole content of Jesus' teaching. It would also misread the animus against him, concerning authority, liberty, compassion, universalism and the rest, which was engendered in the real encounter of word with system, of preaching with tradition, that prefaced the clash of final arraignment. It would also be to miss the singlemindedness of Jesus, the inner consistency of Messianic interpretation as the conflicts deepened.

For it is here that we must locate the inner secret. Why was it that Jesus saw things this way, when almost unanimously his culture and time, his disciples and his foes, saw everything differently? It is true there were the anticipations of a suffering servant within the Divine economy and there is textual evidence that from these Jesus drew something of his own guidance and solace.[1] But they seem to have had little weight and were often re-written in the reverse of their original intention, so as to transfer opprobrium and affliction from the servant to the enemy.[2] Furthermore, the suffering servant of the prophets had surely to be contrasted with the Messiah himself? The disciples themselves, in the Gospels, seem to have made very little of the predictions of Jesus about humiliation and death. Perhaps they thought he meant to convey to them that victory would incur adversity. Perhaps they meant by their incredulity to keep this adversity to their part of the enterprise, that he might go unscathed. This would certainly fit a popular Messianic loyalty, which would aim at all costs to have the central figure inviolate by the expendability of the followers. When he made it clear that the prospect of suffering was for him most of all, they were the more at a loss to know what, in such a philosophy, 'following' could mean. For without a secure Messiah what could be achieved on his behalf?

This consideration explains, not simply the final scattering of the disciples, but also the inner nature of the mind of Jesus. For him, the redeeming efficacy lay, not in an endurance which could battle resentfully through hostility until the tables could be turned, but in the quality of a love that, forbearing enmity, bore the shame and so bore away the wrong. Suffering was not seen by him as a stage necessary to reversal of fortune, but itself, already, the very stuff of the victory. It is in this mind that Christian faith has learned to identify the pattern of truth itself and it calls Jesus 'Son of the Father' in this sense and with this intent. Sonship is not just a proposition about him, needing to be metaphysically

[1] There is, for example, a marked verbal echo of Isa. liii. 3 and Mark ix. 12 in the phrase 'set at nought'. See M. D. Hooker, *Jesus and the Servant*, London, 1959, for a contrary view. The subject is vast and complicated. But if we are to deny any relevance to Jesus' decision of the servant tradition in Isaiah, we simply have two closely parallel themes whose affinity is undeniable whatever has to be said about their disconnection.

[2] See T. W. Manson, *Jesus the Messiah*, London, 1943.

argued, debated and dissected. It is first and essentially an achievement of the spirit in which we learn to recognize the nature of
God. The definitions, as far as they are feasible, then become no
more than the house of intellectual formulation in which its reality
is denoted and made traditionally communicable. That 'the
Father sent the Son' is the confessional expression of love in its
self-authentication, its being and its doing. Jesus is the Son in
being the servant. The Messianic consciousness and the filial are
one. By his patient acceptance of the Jewish antagonism, the
Roman injustice, the national rejection, the disciples' failure, as
these were shaped into the Cross, he accomplished for them a
salvation which left no element outside its reach of pardon and
reconciliation. The sonship is its source and impulse and is most
surely recognizable, not through speculative theology giving it
definition, but in its own cry, 'Father, forgive them; they know
not what they do.'

Christianity has been too often mistaken by outsiders and
diverted from within by reason of its prolonged concern with
metaphysical status. The systematization of theology is no more
than the form in which the living meaning of the history is
symbolized and its witness conserved. It lives by its Christology
but only by a Christology that lives in the pattern and achievement of Jesus as the Christ. All else is comprehended there, because
there an inclusive event is discernible in which God deals with
men in the most elemental areas of their humanity, in their
yearning and their wilfulness.

'SONS OF YOUR FATHER'

The foregoing is the definitive side of Christian faith, the Gospel,
one might say, in the indicative. But it is complemented in the
imperative, through which experience takes up history and parti-
cipates in its meaning. The sonship of Jesus invites to imitation, in
the sense of kindling to the teaching but, more, of receiving the
enabling. The New Testament, through all its diverse witness in
Gospels, Acts and Epistles, sees it this way. 'To as many as
received him, to them he gave the right (or the privilege) to

become the sons of God, to those, that is, who believe on his name.' This reproduces the openness we have already noted in the teaching. 'As many as received him.' There are here no prior qualifications of race, sex, people or condition. The one condition, namely faith, is universally accessible. This community in Messiah is certainly heir to the vocations understood in the old covenant, namely to be truly the possession and delight of God, to minister to the world, to show forth the Divine praise and to fulfil the Divine errands. But it is no longer racial, ethnic or national. It is constituted by the crisis of grace within the option of the person, not by the sanction of power or the will of privacy. It has to do with a birth 'not of blood, nor of the will of the flesh, nor of the will of man'.

'There is no human nature, because there is no God to have a conception of it' Sartre once wrote, in his darkest mood. We might put the Christian meaning if we turned both halves into the affirmative. In simple terms, the Christian experience of man has to do with an experience of family. We exist in being loved, in being related, and that, not merely within the immediate circle of our kin or of our time, but in the totality of meaning. Our humanity consists in the love of God. It is the experience of a relationship which, while it may be glimpsed and learned in the natural order, has so to speak 'conceived' us (in the sense Sartre states in his negation), thought us into life and disclosed and achieved those thoughts in the one whom, for that reason, we call 'the Son of the Father'. 'God loves, and so I am', we might almost say, but having also as intermediate truth 'God loves and so Christ is, and so, through Christ, am I'.

The privilege of man, according to the Gospel, is, then, this mediation of the nature of God in assimilable terms, the apprehension of a family status through the renewing experience of the Divine Name. As such, it fills the goal of the Torah, as Jewry receives it, but does so without the blight of meritoriousness and the confines of a single nation. For the covenantal of Judaism and the political of Islam it offers the filial, as being the final form of the intention of monotheistic religion. Not 'as the seed I am', nor 'in the strength I am', but 'in the Son I am'. It is deeply in debt to the Hebraic for the whole concept of the Messianic, and it is urgently related to the Islamic in its concern for the Divine glory. But it revolutionizes the Messianic assumptions as generally received among their first heirs and it believes that statehood, as the agent of Divine sovereignty, can only relatively serve the absolutes it invokes.

This is not, of course, to claim that empirical Christianity has not in fact often reproduced almost completely the characteristics which its essential Gospel claims to transcend in both the other faiths. Its all too ready ecclesiasticisms and institutional self-interests have acquired aggressive identities often far more stubborn and threatening than those of Old Testament election. It has frequently embraced forms of political expression as pretentious as any in history. The question how these aberrations arose cannot be refused. But if their repudiation is to be right it must return, as all assessments about faiths, to the criteria of their origin and their essential nature. And this, in Christianity, brings us back to sonship, Christ's and ours.

Let it do so with the aid of the familiar parable of the two sons, the parable, so called, of the prodigal son. It is, with telling simplicity, a study in contrasts: elder and younger; home and abroad; famine and feast; husks and bread; 'Father, give me . . .' and 'Father, make me . . .'; 'this thy son', and 'this thy brother'. Within these contrasts the story may be said to comprise the Christian account of human experience and to do so all the more pointedly for its directness and sureness of touch.

It begins with the natural sonship and the sense of 'property', of man as participating in a material inheritance in a context of relatedness—man with the right to ownership, standing in the sequence of the generations, awaiting from the past and expecting towards the future. This is, plainly, the elemental 'caliphate' in parable form, man in physical birth and economic possession. 'Father, give me the portion that is mine.' Then comes the theme of alienation and self-centredness. Estrangement arises from the acquisitive instinct and the inner rejection of the family meaning.

Self-sufficiency takes its journey into distant territory in an inclusive will to separation—from family, environment, the past, and the heritage, insofar as it cannot be portably identified with the self that travels. The relationships are all physically sundered: property is exclusified and for the time being sustains a successful isolation. Then the descent into frustration and despair—the pseudo-friends, the hunger and the swine and the tragic discovery: 'No man gave unto him'.

In this extremity, the recollected home, the bread, the servants and the father, and in that faint rekindling of relationship the man is 'lost enough to find himself again'. 'I will arise and go.' He saw himself as having forfeited sonship, yet spoke of returning to his father. Both sides of the paradox are vital. He 'came to himself' in the double sense as being and yet not being what, or who, he was. Yet somehow his not being so retained the possibility of action as if he were. 'I am no more worthy to be called your son', he would say. The name had been disowned, but the relationship persisted, and strongly enough to sustain a venture into hope. He was confessing as it were the logic of his own unhappy reduction to the miserable cash-nexus of the swine-herd, but saw it better sought in the framework of the life he had abandoned at the start. Destitution, it is true, compelled him. But there was something 'essential' about the terms of his confession: 'I have sinned against heaven and to your face', though he had been oblivious of both.

The narrative shifts then to the old house. The father's welcome is in terms of sonship, not employment. It is spontaneous and unstinted. The robe, the shoes, the ring, the calf—all are to tell his restoration. The father has been long awaiting this return, looking for it 'a great way off'. Sonship is renewed and enlarged in the new dimension of acceptance and delight. Then the contrast—the elder brother refuses to share the family joy or recognize the wanderer. He protests the contrast—'the fatted calf' killed for this bohemian and never 'a kid' for the rigorous, painstaking, sombre loyalist. Was he not working off a grudge on his father? Could it be that he was ever denied a kid for a feast? Was it not rather that in a moment of revelation he perceived he had no friends? that, in his self-sufficiency, he was one of those 'for whom nothing has ever happened'? Had he been cut off from reality in a dreary routine of duty and self-pity, and was thus totally unready for the new dimension of forgiveness and life out of death?

'How can we fail to celebrate this happy day', said the father. But the elder son is adamant and will not go in. 'This thy son' is the only formula he will use: 'call him your son if you will, he is not my brother', he seems to say, while the father gently urges on him his own unbroken quality of relationship: 'This thy brother was dead and is alive again'.

Here, in this simple detail, almost too gentle to be noticed, lies in fact the clue to the whole secret of the restoration. Here too the whole meaning of 'atonement'. For that unbroken relationship, on the father's part, is clearly the only basis of the son's return. If he cannot say within himself 'My father . . . I will arise and go', there is no hope or meaning in his self-discovery. Yet that unchanged image has only stayed so by dint of pain and sorrow. Had the father cursed, disowned, repudiated him, banished the thought of him, or vowed revenge, there could be no returning. Yet these are the only alternatives which could have evaded or smothered or avoided the grief. Precisely in that he does not sever the bonds, the father continues to suffer. That continuity of suffering is then the ground and price of restoration.

There stands then a sort of cross at the heart of the story. The capacity to love is the capacity to bear, and so, in turn, the capacity to suffer. The same events are like one coin, carrying a double impress. What is known to the boy as self-will and misery, is known to the father as brokenheartedness and yearning. The estrangement and the reconciliation, both, are relational. The tie that rebinds, is the tie that holds and love is its cost. The parable, it is true, does not and cannot say all in its one analogy. But the Cross is plainly there. Although the father does no more than wait, his waiting contains within its will to welcome back the son a whole potential of activity and enterprise which, in another context (like the adjacent parables of lost silver and lost sheep), would readily have journeyed to where the husks are. But here the son's own person must be respected even in his enmity. There are, it is true, many situations in which the 'far country' of alienation where the self languishes is not physically remote, as in the parable, but on the common highway of society, in the congestion of the world. Then the father's hospitality can act as well as wait. But either way there is expenditure by which it saves. What this means in one inclusive sign the Christian faith has learned to identify in Christ crucified.

From this redemptiveness springs the invitation to community in its likeness and this is the nature of the Church in its New Testament origin. The father in the parable instinctively desires a fraternity about repentance. The ground in family relation is already there: 'this thy brother' is a truth of flesh. Whatever the personal, or racial, history of the members the common family character of humanity persists. The law is also there, since the temper of the younger son's return fulfils its righteousness in acknowledging his shame. Both these, the natural bond and the moral victory, the father greets in joy and invites the elder son to do the same, pleading against the rupture of the sense of single birth and against the hard insistence of a rigorous view that will not see that in coming to himself the wrongdoer has embraced the law's account of his sin. This being patterned according to the father is the very calling of the Church whose business, in joy, is to be the common society of men in birth and in grace. It is also in both its elements the meaning of the imitation of Christ, in whom faith sees a sharing of our human community and a bearing of our human sin and, by both acts, reconciling men to God and to themselves and giving that reconciliation its self-perpetuating sphere in new community.

Such *imitatio Christi* is the inward counterpart of what Christianity knows historically as the Incarnation. The term has aroused endless, and largely needless, impatience or disquiet among both Jews and Muslims, as being allegedly incompatible with Divine majesty and unity. Neither are in question. It is not that God is less One, only more manifestly so; not less great, but only differently greater. The human calling to bear the Divine Name is seen to be reciprocal to the Divine will to participation with men. 'The Word made flesh' is the point of inter-section. The Christian sees humanity incorporate, not simply in the 'one blood of all nations' in the natural order, but in the reconciling intention of God through 'the body of Christ'. The principle by which we are called to live, namely in redemptive acceptance of our fellows, we have already ourselves discovered in God's dealings with ourselves. The pattern of interhuman relations in forgiveness has its prototype in the Divine undertaking of our situation which we experience in Christ. Or in the familiar saying of Augustine: 'The Son of God became the son of man, that the sons of men might become the sons of God'.

This sonship with Christ is not rightly understood if it is seen only as a kind of loyalty to his teaching. It is also, and more, an energy of his Spirit at work in the mind and the will to reproduce within discipleship the fashion of the Lord. The Holy Communion, as we will notice briefly in the other context of Chapter VII, is central to this theme and stands for that reason at the centre of Christian worship. Not the recital of the law, or the celebration of a city, but a holy table, is the focal point of Christian community as at once receiving and offering in 'the body and the blood' the hospitality of God.

Without straining its simplicity we find in this way in the parable of the son, lost and found, of his rights, his wrongs and his restoration, the epitome of the Christian understanding of man and his privilege—his privilege to inherit, to possess, to err, to pervert, to repent, to return, to find and be found, to love and be loved, to know and to share the reconciliation with God.

'WAITING FOR THE SONS . . .'

It remains to try and relate this core of the Christian, human theme to the questions it incurs by the different emphases of the Jewish, the Islamic and the secular. The danger of venturing the distillation of a large, diverse, long storied thing like Christianity into a single simplicity like that of the parable is obvious. It has to be attempted. But even within its own range there are uneasy questions suggesting themselves to the curious or the insistent. What, for example, of the far country itself, of the sharks waiting for the unwary inheritance, of the cruel cash-nexus which allows the degradation of labour, of farm hands left to the husks of the pigs? What, too, of the elder brother's unyielding opposition? Does not the story, in a way, end in defeat? Even this most exemplary father is left fruitlessly 'entreating' when the narrative concludes. Obduracy, it seems, has the last word.

It may be possible, even proper, exegetically, to silence these questions by the plea that parables have explicit purposes and that we cannot hold them to obligations wider than their central lessons. One cannot illuminate repentance and reconciliation and at the same time cope with all the social and economic problems which proliferate around the turning soul and the family joy. We may note, perhaps, if we are ingenious, that the servants of the father's house seem contented enough and that their conditions look ideal from the 'far country'. But the point, though fair enough, is extraneous and the marginal questions persist, and, what is even more important, the fact that the story makes them marginal.

It is just here that the doubts of Jews and Muslims would arise. Is not this whole Christian concern with man in sonship to God too personal, too private, too 'romantic', too impractical a posture for the real world? Are we not in fact compelled by realism to see the human meaning defined and actualized in more 'public', more institutional, more dominating forms than this ideal of 'sonship'? Must we not locate it squarely within the ethnic or the national? Are not these realities of birth and kindred tougher custodians of whatever we mean by the rule of good than the idealized supra-racial thing we call the Church? Or, better, ought not the sovereignty we believe about God to find its instrument in a correlative earthly sovereignty, established and accepted as its norm and deputy? If 'His state is kingly', then must not His kingship mean a state? Can we have in practicable terms what we call the theological unless we locate it in the political?

Are we not reinforced in these suspicions by the very fact that, historically, Christianity itself has confessed the force of them by capitulating, or freely turning, to these alternatives? The Church, for all its brave Gospel about a universal sonship and a supra-racial family, has in fact allowed history to give it sharply national form and deeply cultural monopoly by race. Are not long stretches of 'the new covenant' as privately ethnic as the old? Are there not whole eras of the Christian Church, both eastern and western, Constantinian and Roman, Byzantine and Lutheran, taking a fully Islamic character vis-à-vis the political order? Is not the doctrine of the two realms a sort of Meccan/Medinan theme without a Hijrah?

It must be so conceded. Nor does Christian faith mean that these great 'principalities', these organs of human existence, as it calls them, are in any way negligible or irrelevant. On the contrary, it acknowledges their irreducible role in the order of the human world and gives them relative and due validity within the larger whole. But, when it is true to its Gospel, it does not entrust them with the whole onus of the Divine kingdom. It sees the state as holding the ring for the inward forces of righteousness, attaining, or at least attempting, such justice as its nature allows, within which other instruments of truth and value may undertake their inalienable tasks. It sees nationhood as, likewise, a necessary context and sanction of the good life, but not itself the crux, still less the guarantor, of it. Political kingdoms and popular identities, the realms of power and blood, are inescapable factors with which it is imperative to reckon, both as proper agents and menacing rivals of men's final loyalty under God. But there must always be, not only with them, but strenuously over against them, the rights of God as the only true condition of man. The whole essence of the Christian distinctiveness, in new testament for old, in the Cross not the Hijrah, in the counter choice that both salutes and rejects the Jewish and the Islamic, lies in this conviction of sonship, in nature and through grace, as the ultimate religious experience.

That conviction brings us to three final reflections and to the

quotation from St Paul borrowed at the head of these paragraphs
from the great eighth Chapter of the Epistle to the Romans, with
its picture of the 'whole creation . . . waiting for the revealing of
the sons of God'. These have to do with the personal, the tragic
and the expectant. Christian faith stands or falls by its commitment to the person. Persons, not individuals: for it is only by
statistical criteria that the latter exist. Persons are constituted in
community and, through the personal, the racial, the economic,
the social, the political, have their meaning. There are of course
strong temptations to reverse this dictum and to find the personal
dimension meaningless *except* as a unit within these larger ends.
Inter-penetration there obviously is: but the Christian faith is
pledged and bound over to the conviction that the personal must
be paramount in their interpretation and their forms.

There are, it is true, many factors in science and literature,
telling, as we have seen, against this belief in the significance of
the person. We have to be warned that all we think and postulate,
as well of course as what we see and register, is conditioned by
ourselves as thinking it and its 'interiority' though inescapable
may have no relation to what really is outside this anthropocentric
knowing of it. But the point is academic, since the alternative
'truth' is unattainable: and it is worth noting that it is we ourselves who are alert enough not only to appreciate, but to origi-
nate, the warning. These niceties aside, the real world of our
destiny and of our being, not to be eluded or illusioned by how it
might be if we were not ourselves, abides with us and we in it.
The significance of the personal cannot be denied: it can only be,
either violated, or accepted. It is irreducible. Reality, in the
Christian view, has to do, not finally with nations, or lands, or
goods, or forces, or laws, or techniques, or ideas, or power, or
politics, but with people in all these, and beyond them, capable of
being victims, alienated, frustrated, exiled, bartered, depraved or
deprived, but capable also of being victors, loved, articulate,
creative, compassionate, responsible, free and alive. For such is
'the adoption of sons'.

But a humanity conceived within the priority of the personal is necessarily seen in the proportions of tragedy. It is this attention to suffering which, it may be soberly said, is the characteristic alertness of the Christian Gospel. Aspects of this were anticipated in the discussion earlier of Abraham. It is a quality which readers of the Qur'ān find singularly lacking in the traditional Islamic scheme of things. It is as if the whole logic of Islam, in its formative history, wills to exclude the tragedy of man. Success and vindication are its goals and treasure. Endurance, certainly, is there and a fine quality of tenacious courage against odds. Nor in the living, dying world, has Islam escaped the mysteries of creature-hood, of death and transience. For these it has a noble dignity. Its own tensions have given rise, in the Shī'ah form, to apprehensions of suffering as marking, rather than just impeding, the designs of God. But these are not central or definitive. Islam, as we have sought to show, is a theology of uncompromised majesty and unambiguous victory.

It is different with Jewry and the Christian faith acknowledges a large debt both to the great Old Testament prophets and to the sustained acceptance of the world's contumely which Judaism has patiently suffered and to which Christendom itself has grievously contributed. Such history makes easy verdicts intolerable and broad ones impossible. Yet there remains about Jewish heroism a provocation of exclusivism. It is too often a suffering against, rather than for or with, humanity and, though perversely, its own particularism has served to excite it. In this dark sphere the Christian mind goes back, as a needle to its north, to the Messianic decision of Jesus for the Cross and finds in that embracing of sorrow a rejection by, but also of, the ethnic, communal norm of the Old Testament. The subsequent majority exemption of Jewry, by its own decisions, from those choices and from their universal consequence in the New Testament, confirms the association between suffering and privacy that may be read throughout Hebrew history.

The Christly dimension allows the veritable tragedy of the human condition and sets itself to undertake its saving. It re-cognizes that the privilege of man includes this self-damnation, that sons possess their possessions and in so doing forfeit themselves. It knows that 'the father's house' has a door open not only from but to 'the far country'. For there is no arbitrary inclusion in grace. It allows that sonship only comes to fullness out of crisis, that self-righteousness may so stagnate as to fail to recognize its own end in love. It is aware that conversion needs to be endlessly renewed in every generation and that there is no cumulative remedy for that world of alienation into which the wanderer strays and 'no man gives'. Its furniture may change with the centuries and slums displace the sties. But callousness finds new forms. This is not to exonerate the social conscience but only to confess perpetually the personal crisis and to set regeneration at the heart of man's destiny. The faith of the Cross consists in taking humanity in the deepest terms, and, therefore, unreservedly to incur its tragic quality. Only because it is a tragic reading of the situation is it a great salvation for it.

Here is the third dimension of hope. For it is impatience which loses heart: only the love that 'endureth all things' can also hope them. Law and merit cannot really admit of completely new beginnings. For they 'require—or retain—what is past'. The political answer too, however maximized, leaves unprobed and unanswered the range of evil that eludes its competence or accompanies its processes. The very realism which is its strength confesses a partiality when tested by the patterns of sonship and grace. Its part in the sovereignty of God and the achievement of the human meaning is relative to goals beyond its own contriving. We shall only finally justify hope where we truly measure despair. The sonship which identifies our exile and our folly is the one sure ground of our being in truth.

So the Christian faith looks in all men for the transactions of sonship to God and, for its own part, finds them mediated and achieved through the meaning, within our common humanity, of the sonship of Jesus, from whom it takes not simply the criterion of what we must be, but the energy by which we may. 'To become the sons of God' is the truly human charter, radical and disturbing, but real and actual.

From these three measures of the human privilege, Hebraic, Islamic and Christian, in their classic character, we pass to issues of the contemporary scene which might seem to call them all in total question.

VII

'Bad Faith'

'A KIND of world view facilitating, supporting and even furthering, man's evasion and escape.' So runs the familiar indictment of religious faith as made by a whole variety of contemporary writers in the secularist and existential tradition. The words, however, are Karl Barth's in his *Church Dogmatics*, where, in the fourth volume, he reproaches the external acceptance and the outward motions of belief as disowning and disarming its real meaning.

The most cunning of all the stratagems which the resisting element in man can use in self-defence against the word of grace is simply to immunize, to tame and to harness. It is politely to take its seat in the pew, cheerfully to don the vestment and mount the pulpit, zealously to make Christian gestures and movements, soberly to produce theology, and in this way, consciously participating in the confession of Jesus Christ, radically to ensure that his prophetic work is halted . . .[1]

Barth's intention, of course, is to expose what by the criteria of the Gospel he sees as 'bad faith', in order by this chastening and honesty to effectuate a true believing integrity and a genuine worship. Kierkegaard had said much the same with even more devastating scorn a century earlier in his attack on Christendom, as being, for him, the externalized travesty of Christian discipleship.

Sartre, Camus, Beckett and a score of others would say that their purpose is foredoomed, that their assumption of a feasible, religious integrity is untenable. There may be links of admiration, and even a residual community of inspiration, between interior, Christian repudiations of religious self-deception, and the total religious negation of the secularizers. But in essence they are irreconcilable. For the one, 'bad faith' is a symptom, a temptation, a

---

[1] Karl Barth, *Church Dogmatics*, Vol. iv, Pt. 3, first half, translated by G. W. Bromiley, Edinburgh, 1961, p. 259.

distortion, within an utterly authentic standing, and can only be pilloried as such. For the other, 'bad faith' is an inherent and implicit quality of the religious dimension itself, seeing that all 'faith' is essentially wishful, and, once we are really alert to the fact, there is no ultimate honesty feasible within theological belief. Faced with infinity, we have nothing more than the human affinity and to want more, irrespective of how loyally or how corruptly we seek or find it, is itself a treachery to life.

The hope of this Chapter, taking a point of departure by deliberate intention from this suggestive ambiguity in the usage of 'bad faith', is to face the issue whether the human privilege, as now considered within three religious structures, is not an illusory pretension, a pretentious illusion. Are these beliefs about man in Judaism, Islam and Christianity, alike a timid dishonesty that will not face the real void? Having set out, as we did in Chapter I, from man in possession and dispossession, in undeniable empire and in oppressive disquiet, have we in fact returned where we started, informed perhaps, but hardly satisfied, by a survey of obsolescent credulity in the guise of Semitic optimism? 'You have the sadness of one who has set out to go very far and ends up by finding himself where he began', says a character in Ignazio Silone's *A Handful of Blackberries.* 'Didn't they teach you at school that the world is round?' Have we made a merely academic detour through the Bible and the Qur'ān to arrive at the lethal conclusion that their notions of humanity, however central to race, power and suffering, are nevertheless vitiated by their evident comfort and discredited by their impossible assurance? What has Jewish, Muslim, Christian confidence about the human dignity to say, what can it say, to the total modern disqualification of man as meant for religion?

The first part of the answer may well set out from the coincidence already before us, namely that 'bad faith' is identified by belief within belief, and that it is allegedly inseparable from belief itself. For between these two incompatible positions there is a clear conviction in common, namely a responsibility in man for ultimacy. In the one case it summons faith to a constant self-awareness lest it be self-deceived: in the other the core of self-awareness is that faith *is* self-deceived. The one is, as it were, a positive vigilance, the other a negative. But at least they are alike in requiring of man a responsible relation to himself, not merely *within* a framework of ultimate reference, but *with* it. They are akin in demanding that man be obligated about illusion, and that without limit of protective conformity or quiescent tradition or comforting practice or orthodox shelter. It is just this inclusive demand which we shall take in conclusion as the surest token of the privilege for which we are arguing in the human condition. The immediate point is simply to see that there is no necessary, if there is often an actual, immunity from this ultimate self-questioning in the religious, as popularly contrasted with the existential, attitude of man. Or, putting the matter the other way round, if we are to demand 'good faith'—and this would seem the conclusion if, with Sartre we are to deplore 'bad faith'—then there is no necessary compulsion to abandon the religious dimension in doing so. For the religious temper is well able to venture against itself the questions that take it into total jeopardy. The fact that it does so from a point of departure and of return that is dogmatic does not necessarily mean any final reservation of an ultimate risk of losing all. While faith has often justly incurred the reproach of timidity or complacence, we have of late had too much of the allegation that it has no honest will to let reality disprove it. On the contrary: if men are seeking for the easier options they are not all on the side of faith. A sturdy will not to be deceived is no monopoly of the despairers. Sincerity, of course, is doubtless feasible in many realms both of belief and unbelief. It is not of this we speak, but rather the integrity of an unreserved responsibility to truth.

Our first business, then, is to note and illustrate the capacity, indeed the impulse, within religious faiths to reckon with themselves radically, to be totally in trust with themselves, as distinct from a mere conformist or quiescent situation of belief. We must take the significance of the fact that 'bad faith' is an inward judgement, deeply and passionately made, from time to time, from the heart of dogma and discipleship themselves. In part, it was there that the exterior critics learned their existential concern for integrity—the concern they find themselves constrained to turn against the whole religious sphere. The purpose of this exposition is to assess both sides of this pursuit of unreserving openness, whether for or against belief, whether inside or outside faith, whether towards God in man or man alone. From these two themes in their relation, the third readily follows, namely the implications of both as a commentary on the whole autonomy of man. This is the relevance of the 'bad faith' issue to the entire thesis of Semitic religions in respect of man. If it is seen that the human crisis, whether in religion or in religionlessness, is a total crisis consciously to be taken as such, that conclusion surely underlines and confirms the Hebrew, Muslim, Christian measure of the human caliphate as we have explored it. We may then discover that the deepest 'bad faith' of all is neither the escapism into subservience alleged of religious attitudes, nor the willed illusion of meaning that the existentialists abjure, but rather the refusal of the conjoined vocation to take up a whole and to consecrate a whole, which we have understood as man's in the mastery and the creaturehood for which he is made.

No attempt is made in this context to study the whole mystery of evil in the abstract, nor to engage the discussion in the characteristic tenets of the three faiths in this field. This may seem to some a serious incompleteness. But our duty is to the great positive of man's autonomous stature under God, with the human authority over nature and the ethnic, political and filial forms of its expression in the threefold Semitic understanding. The argument can properly concentrate on this without diverting itself into a whole theology of evil, or a philosophy of evil, and without staying to theorize about free will and providence. This is not to ignore the dark shadows of perversity and pride that attend the whole human prerogative. Our need, however, in this context, is to take them within the affirmative calling, or, in doctrinal terms, to see the fall within creation and not as its undoing. To see the faiths in radical accusation, whether from within or from without, will bring us close to the reality of evil. It is in fact already implicit in the earlier

analysis of the perpetual temptation to make absolute what is
relative, and to enthrone what is tributary. Hebrew, Muslim and
Christian attitudes to power, or community, or vital interest disclose it unmistakeably. The necessity, and the capacity, to say:
'This is bad faith' will be, for present purposes, a sure enough
index to the nature of sin, and all the better for its concreteness.

The task, then, in what follows is to study the significance of
'bad faith' as an inward judgement and as an outward charge,
and, in the light of these, to proceed beyond them to the ultimate
'bad faith' of caliphal man as he is defined in previous chapters.[1]

'BAD FAITH': THE INWARD JUDGEMENT

We must keep, of course, the saving grace of humour. Our exposition has to do with the radical self-deception, the decisive
disloyalty, of the religious temper, wherever it takes shape.
There are manifestly many easy-going, even comic, foibles, of
religious man, hypocrisies, frailties, insincerities, which, though
they may deepen into more sinister proportions, need first a
tolerant sympathy. *The Thousand and One Nights*, that storehouse
of human roguery, is full of them, Or there is the benign and
playful Chaucer, with his classic human canvas of pilgrims to
Canterbury. 'Pleasant was his absolution' he wrote of the Friar . . .

> . . . an easy man to give penance,
> There as he wist to have a good pittance:
> For unto a poore order for to give
> Is signe that a man is well y shrive . . .
> For many a man so hard is of his heart
> He may not weep although him sorë smart.
> Therefore, instead of weeping and prayeres,
> Men must give silver to the poorë freres.

As a butt of kindly humour, all this, and its like, deserves a gentle
irony. It is not these half playful, even engaging, incongruities of
religious life, that are in mind. There is little point in censure that
has not wit enough first to be amused. These are but the surface

---

[1] A certain problem of phrasing arises here from the ambiguity of prepositions,
'in' and 'of' after 'faith'.

eddies of human nature. Far beyond and below them is the real business with which, for example Kierkegaard, has to do, the charge of a thoroughgoing perversion of belief. Alms and the man in some discrepancy, as Chaucer satirizes it, or even cash in lieu of conscience, are minor tricks of compromise. Forms of faith as unfaith, the use of God to evade God—these are the serious measures of deception, and within them man bringing with his disloyalty the pretension or the pretence that it is otherwise, as a sort of inverted tribute to his proper calling.

God against 'God' is the theme that stirs the Hebrew Scriptures to their most passionate eloquence. There is no element in their ultimate faith which is exempt from the radical arraignment of the prophetic spirit. Sacrifice and Zion, election and the land, the fathers and the covenant—all are explicitly declared forfeit if they no longer ring true in the soul of the nation. In the most scornful irony, Isaiah inveighs against his people as 'rulers of Sodom and men of Gomorrah' and sweeps away the whole sacrificial system as never intended (Isa. i. 10–15). Amos, likewise, calls in question the wilderness period as ever having been a tutelage in rites and offerings (Amos. v. 21–5). History, in these terms, is undone and reversed, only because authenticity is forsaken by its heirs. Nothing is sacrosanct without integrity. In the hands of Amos the very notion of election becomes itself the sentence of national disqualification, witness the eloquent indictment by which the opening chapters arraign the surrounding heathen peoples, as all Israel might approve, only to reach in devastating climax the repudiation of Israel itself. In Jeremiah, the grim register of popular apostasy holds, in the prophet's inner fidelity, what may well be described as the profoundest religious rejection of religion in all history.

Indeed, it constitutes the sort of judgement of religion which only religion can attain. It is just here, in parenthesis, that the fallacy of the contemporary cult of 'religionlessness' occurs. For if we fail to reserve the ultimate dimensions that worship affirms we have neither ground nor means to correct their perversion. We cannot well reproach the easy, complacent service of sanctuaries unless the sanctities abide beyond them. The perils of religiosity, so vigorously exposed as the death warrant of the 'God' they 'ungodly' intend, are only truly identified and overcome in the authentically religious. A call to behave 'as if God is dead' is no salvation from the worship of a god who is already so: only the recovery of the worthy sense of the God who is alive. We cannot both correct the religious temper and dispense with it: only by worship can worship be purged: only if we preserve the horror of a final blasphemy can we recognize and defeat the lesser hypocrisies. There is in all Biblical literature no more anti-religious figure than Jeremiah, for the reason that there is none more loyally religious. Secularism may sharply expose and castigate the viciousness of much religion. But the recovery of true religion can, plainly, never be a secularist achievement.

That reflection aside, the essential point here, emerging from Hebrew prophecy, is this capacity to be critically against the thing itself in the very name of it. Being against 'God' on behalf of God, as are these great protagonists of the Hebraic tradition, demonstrates unmistakeably that their faith is not some trap of false transcendence. Rather a self-disqualifying ability lives at the very core of its ultimate awareness of God and it is able to reject all the elements of its religious fulfilment—sacrifice, covenantal standing, kingship, ritual, feasts and fasts, indeed all the forms of godwardness—which might be assumed to have acquired, by virtue of their relation to the absolute allegiance, an immunity from question and from blame, the sort of immunity, that is, which, were it allowed, would for ever atrophy and pervert the faith that approved it. Power, it is said, corrupts, and the more totally the more it is total. There is a comparable situation about worship and the claims of faith. Serving the ultimacy of God they tend to take their own for granted. Being in the courts of the Lord would seem to be the place most right for congratulation. Religion, therefore, is open to the perpetual temptation to become the absolute it acknowledges, to arrogate the worth it celebrates. Impatiently identified, this menace generates, along with other factors, the will to secularity, the demand for a religionless condition. But this is only to exchange a perverted, but still retrievable, perspective in ultimacy, for one that is at best a law unto itself. It is in this sense that it takes the religious mind to redeem the religious form. It is where the hazards belong that the salvation must arise.

And arise it does. This is the supreme lesson of Jeremiah and all the prophets, disowning godliness in God's own name and establishing His glory against establishment. The faith of the Old Testament at its deepest is constituted, we might even say, in knowing its own 'bad faith'. The final answer to the external critic is not that he has nothing to say, but that he has nothing to add. The most authentic strictures are already inwardly alive and it is only by inwardness that they can be brought to issue in newness of life. 'Woe unto them that are at ease in Zion', is the language of its own loyalty. Even when, in hardness of heart, it is despised, rejected and silenced, that defiance only deepens the majesty of the reproof and the confession of the crisis:

Let us lie in wait for the righteous man, because he is clean contrary to our doings . . . the very sight of him is a burden to us, because his manner of life is unlike that of others and his ways are strange . . . He boasts that God is his Father. Let us see . . . Let us test him with insults and torture, that we may find out how gentle he is and make trial of his forbearance. Let us condemn him to a shameful death, for according to what he says, he will be protected. Thus they reasoned, but they were led astray . . . and did not know the secret purposes of God.[1]

The community knows its own saviours even when it breaks their hearts, and the saviours, the prophets or the priests, know that their very rejection is the paradox of saving. For by their fidelity to the end they have measured to the full the perversity their righteousness condemns: but in so doing they have loved to the full the calling which that perversity had shamed. These are the transactions of redemption. They are the hallmarks of a religion able to be itself against itself. They are both the tokens and the crisis of the integrity of faith, the living shape of the lordship of God.

[1] Wisd. of Sol. xxii. 12 f.

These self-correcting loyalties even unto death are bequeathed, within Biblical religion, from the Old to the New Testament. Indeed the latter must be seen as the abiding form of what the crisis in the Old demands. In Christianity the historical core of belief has to do with an event which is seen as an inclusive encounter with the pride and waywardness of religion. The faith of the Cross, therefore, is calculated never to be surprised or taken unawares by lengths of human evil. It has seen them all in the crisis of its own genesis. It does not have a theology which has reckoned only partially with the pervertibility of religion and might therefore be either sanguine or dismayed in its presence. This is not to say that Christendom has not reproduced the religious blindness through which its own Cross was reared. On the contrary: it has done so most perversely of all in espousing the dogma and the 'cause' of the very Cross itself—witness the enormities of Anti-Semitism. It has shown a tragic will to 'crucify the Son of God afresh' in the very business of bearing his name. But this tragedy is itself identified as such by the measure of the Cross alone. The passions of men are only fully disqualified in the passion of our Lord. Where the Gospel rules in its true relevance, the Christian faith knows that men have most need of repentance when they can see only self-righteousness. Rightly subdued to the meaning of the Cross, there can be no religious innocence in the awareness of Christianity. There is this perpetual accusation, this sure indictment, of the disloyal in the very texture of the thing confessed. The Cross does not acquiesce to be uncrossed.[1]

---

[1] A phrase, somewhere, of T. S. Eliot. Or compare Robert Frost's poem, 'The Peaceful Shepherd':

> If heaven were to do again . . .
> I should be tempted to forget,
> I fear, the Crown of Rule,
> The Scales of Trade, the Cross of Faith,
> As hardly worth renewal.
> For these have governed in our lives,
> And see how men have warred.
> The Cross, the Crown, the Scales may all
> As well have been the Sword.

Collected Poems, New York, 1949, p. 319.

It is this fact, gathered into the doctrine of the Holy Spirit, which makes the Christian form of the prophetic responsibility for the whole which we have already noted in the Old Testament. The Church is generated by that which forbids it ever to be an end in itself. The servant-status is the form and definition of its relation to the transcendent. Its being is to find identity with the self-offering of the Master. 'It is enough for the servant that he be as his Lord.' This calling is the central meaning of the Holy Communion by which the faith and worship of Christianity are symbolically held in frame. The word and work of Jesus are not to be celebrated by proprietary pride, in ceremonial recitation and possessive acclaim. 'Take and eat this.' The broken body is to be assimilated as the life principle of action with the self, the sign and shape of the claim and the power of love accepted as being at once for us and through us. Men do not rehearse the Sermon on the Mount except in danger of congratulation for its nobility. The sacrament summons them to a living conformity with its translation into the life-situation of the Cross—a situation which has within it all the elements of man's crisis and his restoration.

The cynic may say that Holy Communion is in no way exempt from the liabilities of religion to externality and deception. Perhaps the Holy Communion least of all. He will be right in his contention and only wrong in his cynicism. There are no necessary guarantees, no assured immunities, for the patterns of grace. The faith of the Gospel has no exceptionality preserving it from the besetting evils of all religion. But it does possess in its own unique way the active criterion of its own consistency which has not let it rest. As with the Old Testament, though differently, the truths which condemn it are its own, and, as with the Hebrew prophets, they do so efficaciously. The Christian faith is well able to incriminate, both within itself and in the world around, the temptation to use God in the very act of serving Him. For, at the heart of it, is a service which has no ground nor place except in God's use. The Gospel has to do with a relationship of men to God which is beyond all proximate responsibilities and constitutes as it were a responsibility for responsibility itself.

It may not be so ready a matter to see and express this self-critical quality in Islam. This is partly because of the political extroversion which we noted carefully in Chapter V. The criteria of finality and success, as we saw, tended to generate, if not also to require, a self-vindicating or self-approving temper. The close identity between the will of God and the way of the Prophet, between the purpose in Heaven and the policy in the field, checked, if it did not wholly preclude, the dimension of inward criticism. Vigorous activist religions cannot readily afford either doubt or self-questioning. The political realism which is the very strength and genius of the Islamic way fits ill with disquiet about whether God is with us and whether we are rightly for Him. It is liable to prefer confidence to conscience and to suspect inward mis-giving. The theme of conscience is indeed one on which the Qur'ān keeps a remarkable silence and its concern with suffering is almost wholly limited to incidental fortitude, rather than re-demptive potentiality. From this angle its sense of itself as 'a book in which there is nothing dubious' has a disturbing aspect for minds nurtured in the different ethos of Jeremiah or of Gethsemane.

Nevertheless, there lives at the heart of Islam the obligation to refuse all gods but God and the principle is there more explicit and aggressive than in any other faith. 'That religion may be wholly God's' (Surah 8. 39) is an objective which, admittedly, in context turns on militant action. But it states an end which is capable of being applied in truth against Islam itself. If the outsider can in part see this more readily than the Muslim, this may well be so precisely because of the intensity of the spirit with which it is inwardly held. Islam has no monopoly of the habit by which faiths fail to let their witness tell against their institution. But the potentiality is there and from time to time finds articulate ex-pression. Islam itself may become a substitute for God Himself and do so the more readily for the fact that its own *raison d'être* is to disown all such substitution.

Quranic passages abound which implicitly sustain the duty of self-criticism in radical terms. Aside from *Shirk* itself, the aliena-tion of worship from the true to the false, there is the central theme of *Zulm*, or 'wrong', understood as done against God, the core of which is usurpation by man of what is God's. By its repeated reminder: 'God knows what you conceal in your hearts', the Qur'ān teaches how truth is not mocked, least of all by those who pretend its service or its esteem. Implicit in its vigorous iconoclasm lies the profoundest disqualification of false religion and of pseudo-worship.

It seems fair to see in the whole Ṣūfī, or mystical, tradition within Islam a token of this capacity, in the name of God, to question the establishment that names Him. It needs to be remembered that Sufism has, through long stretches of Islamic history, proved the main bearer of its authentic genius. This is the more remarkable, given the thoroughness of the Islamic system and the rigorous character of its dogmatic structure—factors which might have been expected to deter or defeat the independence of spirit and spontaneity of will by which Sufism emerged and persisted. This is a topic too large and manifold either to discuss or document in this context. But the fact of it sufficiently sustains the only point of immediate concern, namely the ability of Islam to generate a temper able inwardly to set its religious ends against its outward or doctrinal means.

'Islam is almost like a stranger among the Muslims', writes Muḥammad Fāḍil Jamālī, in his *Letters on Islam*,[1] quoting Surah 25. 30, 'The apostle said: O my Lord, truly my people have accounted this Qur'ān a thing discarded'. His argument differs from ours as a more general deploring of Muslim inattention to, or compromise of, Islam. But the implication is capable of even deeper force. The root idea in the term here translated 'discarded' has to do with deliberate neglect, perhaps associated with time, in the sense of obsolescence, or with distaste, in the sense of complacent rejection. Either way, the controversy of the Scripture with the people, of the 'faith' with the 'faithful', abides. This means that Islam, for all its downrightness fortifying its community as an end in itself, is able for their repudiation as no more than nominal adherents.

[1] Translated from the Arabic by the author, London, 1965, p. 90.

In an elaborate, and in places highly assertive, analysis, Ismāʿīl Rāgī al-Fārūqī, in 'Urūbah and Religion, has recently distinguished five different meanings to the term Islām. It is firstly, and in crucial definition: '. . . God's will, i.e. values as members of their hierarchical realm related to one another in such order as God has dictated . . . Islam is a body of values constituting an ideal realm, a transcendant supernal plenum of value at the center of which stands God.' But it is, further and secondly, the ideal Shariʿah, or sacred law, 'discernible and realizable by men but never exhaustively discerned or realized'. The actual response of Muslims in history is the third meaning, the 'consensus and practice of the adherents of the faith'. Fourthly, between the Shariʿah and the Ummah, the ideal 'ought-to-be' and the actual community achievement, stands the Sunnah of Muḥammad, being both actual and ideal, in history and yet of eternity, 'the perfect actualization of the ideal'. Fifthly, Islam is 'the stream of being which, activated and led by the Prophet in the seventh century, has grown into a community and a history, endowed with distinctive ideology and institutions'.[1]

Insofar as this schematization is operative—and there are many echoes of it in less sophisticated form—it witnesses to an inward, if often only theoretical, responsibility of empirical Islam to authentic Islam. 'Bad faith', then, here also, is not an indictment which could only occur to an outsider. It is an accusation which belongs with the interior awareness of the faith itself. In its own way, Islam is calculated, as Judaism and Christianity are, to disavow itself in being itself, to hold its meaning against its practice. The fact that in the defensive and aggressive mentality of its present history, this capacity may be at a discount ought not to obscure either its depth or its potential.

It follows, then, that secular charges of 'bad faith', arising externally to these three religions, may be at once received and rejected—received in that they speak with no strange voice, rejected in that their point is already taken without their conclusion. The very temptations of the faiths, as we have earlier reviewed

[1] Amsterdam, 1962, pp. 200–2.

them, in their interior recognition as temptations, make it clear
that the ultimates they serve are not self-imprisoned. Monotheism,
as here understood, is not conceived as a self-absolutizing allegiance immune from disloyalty. For it is only entrusted with truth:
and truth in trust exempts its bearers least of all. Hebrew prophecy
denying an inviolate Zion, Christian discipleship striving against
Christendom, Muslim reproach of Islam for Islam's sake, are one,
beneath all their disparities, in confessing a supremacy that subdues
their allegiance. It is the living God that makes it so. If His service
is perfect freedom, it is also an eternal vigilance.

But this ability to know its own 'bad faith'—though deeply
relevant to the outward accusations against belief—does not of
itself dispose of their contention. We have to take the significance
we are arguing further into the realm of the contemporary disquiet
if we are to reckon with it fully.

'BAD FAITH': BELIEVING IN UNBELIEF

'Atheism', wrote Jean Paul Sartre, 'is a cruel, long term business.'[1]
Yet inescapable. For whatever the attractive desirability of faith,
it is in truth illusory, and honesty requires that, however distress-
ingly, it must be abandoned. The situations in modern literature
designed to convey this opinion we have, summarily, noted in
Chapter I. Faith, on this view, is not merely capable of deception
with its authenticity, it is inherently incapable of authenticity. So
regarded, its capacity for self-disqualification in the name of a
truer expression is a meaningless subtlety, inasmuch as belief has
no destiny save entire and irretrievable disqualification. Alert or
obtuse, critical or sanguine, it is all the same. The real awakening
into nothingness evacuates all confidence, whether sensitive or
secure. Faith clings falsely to its hopes only because it cannot bear
the vacuum with which reality confronts our spirits. Religion
prefers an inclusive deception as the price of a tolerable existence,
to an admission that man is pure contingency, with no 'necessity'
about him. All belief, on this reckoning, is the vested interest
either of fear or of perversity: it is a fundamental dishonesty which

[1] In *Words*, translated into English by I. Clephane, London, 1964, p. 171.

will not admit the conspiracy of comforting wishfulness by which it lets itself be fooled.

The earnestness and passion of this contemporary mood must not be lost to sight in any reaction to its dogmatism. For they contain a vital clue. It will be fair to take counsel with its own impulse and question the context of its genesis. If faith may, allegedly, derive from human conditioning against fear, so that we are prone to write the world in the image of our wistfulness, it will not be inconsistent to imagine that unfaith, likewise, may take departure from conditions of circumstance with no better claim to authenticity. Indeed, we have already half seen this happening in the pages of Beckett, Sartre and others, noted in the opening Chapter. It is arguable that the 'void' out of which the unfaith springs is a far less real context than the world of nature, of values and of history, out of which the canons of faith are drawn. Certainly much of the literature that mirrors secular negation is born in the abnormalities of underground resistance movements, of war and devastation, of shell-shock, insanity and deprivation, of bomb craters and violence. It has to do, in large measure, with the exploitation of contemporary technology, with the retreat from nature, from poetry, from human imagination, with the distractions and passivities, the atrophy of vivid and costly relationships, that are the mark of disillusioned society.

It would, of course, be idle utopianism to deny these things, and empty delusion to ignore them. But the crucial question is whether they tell the whole story, and, even more crucial, whether we accept them as the invincible condition of humanity, the definitive verdict on our souls. If we do, then the conclusions drawn from them may be also irreducible. If we do not, then their relevance has to be countered, balanced, redeemed, by the contrasted assurances of meaning, of wonder and of worth that have been, from nature, grace and beauty, the stock-in-trade of generations of artists, poets and lovers, whose agelessness must be strenuously set against the distorted and distorting pre-occupations of our contemporary malaise.

Meanwhile, the very intensity of this will not to be cheated by belief needs to be pondered. For there is a certain circularity about its argument, which makes it promptly suspect. The will to despair accuses religious faith of 'badness' because it cannot accept despair. Yet the one criterion of 'good faith' in this connection is the will to accept despair. It is this which justifies the suspicion that the philosophy of existential dismay is in fact an evasion of the problem of meaning. It would be equally possible to formulate the converse and, taking hope as the corollary of 'good faith', reject all refusal of hope as having betrayed itself in the wilful illusion of insignificance. If the element of will in the will to believe is deceptive and damnable, there is no less an element of will in the will to disbelief, and it must be clear that it is an entirely open option which is to be taken. There may be oppressive circumstances in which the negations are readier and easier than the affirmatives. But there is no finality that may legitimately exclude the alternative. Browning's 'grand perhaps' will always remain, or *Fra Lippo Lippi*'s

> You'll find the soul you've missed within
> yourself,
> When you return Him thanks.

It is just this other possible dimension of life that supplies the different quality of existentialism in Albert Camus, whom it is proposed to take here as a single field for reflection on the paradox of 'unfaith' and integrity, which he exhibits better, for our present concerns, than almost any other writer. He is one with the rest of the school in his ability to communicate the utter loss of meaning and the sense of the absurd. Yet there is that redeeming love of sunlight and the beaches which persists within the gloom of pointlessness and vacancy, and gives birth to his theme of the 'style of life' in which the perspectives of faith may be said to begin, tentatively, to reappear. He knew, of course, the dereliction of humanity. His sensitivity was taught by the mute, patient, inarticulate suffering of his mother, whose silent, uncomplaining tedium gathered into an abiding parable the whole absurdity of life in the world. Yet among the recurrent words of his vocabulary,

12—P.M.

so many of which still characterize the literature of rejection —prison, exile, condemnation, gamble, disease and the rest—he let 'summer' have unwonted place and with it the paradox of joy and sensuous delight. Thus he was able to bestow a 'style' on life which somehow defied its ontological despair. The value of life can never lie in its meaning: for it has none. But it can lie in the way we live it. Sisyphus *wills* his happiness by refusing to let the stone lie at the foot of the hill. Futility, surely, yet refined by the nobility that accepts it. At least he is alive, and present in the earth. If hopelessness be the price of this, courage will pay it. The very incomprehensibility of life, not insulated by pseudo-faith, gains a positive character by the will to live it heroically. It is in this sense that Camus claims there can be no such thing as 'a literature of despair'. The creativity which makes the literature is already beyond the despair, not because it has returned to the cheating faiths, or taken refuge in ontological meaning, but because the creative response surmounts the actual absurdity. 'In the middle of winter', he wrote, 'I learned at last that I carried inside me an invincible summer.'[1] Hence the compassion, the honesty, the directness, of such works as *The Plague* and *The Myth of Sisyphus*. The awareness of beauty in nature, which might so easily prompt a man to turn in nausea away from stricken human nature, could yet be made to sustain a steady effort after 'humanity'. 'Yes! there is beauty and there are the humiliated. Whatever the difficulties of the enterprise may be, I should like to be unfaithful neither to the one nor to the other.'[2]

Camus deserves this extended discussion because he focuses and powerfully exemplifies a quality in this whole movement of thought which seems to lead the observer, if not the sceptic himself, away from the negative of his case to the positive of his concern. Why should the lack of significance be so movingly significant? Why should the loss of meaning be so meaningful? Why

[1] In 'Retour à Tipasa', L'Été, Paris, 1954, p. 158.
[2] *Ibid.,,* p. 160. In *L'Envers et L'Endroit*, and in *Noces*, Camus described the temptation to renounce all effort after an understanding of humanity and to surrender in indifference to the sheer beauty of the earth.

should absurdity command such integrity in its defence? How is it that a world so prone to cheat belief should engender so urgent a will never to be cheated? If meaninglessness is all, need it, could it, be so defiantly embraced? Is there not a sense, as Camus himself hints, in which the style disproves the despair?

It is wise for belief not to make too ready claims about the hidden logic of the unbelievers. 'Lord, I believe: help Thou mine unbelief' is not a prayer that can be put by any on the lips of others. For it is only a personal confession. The fact, however, remains that contemporary novels of disbelief seem strangely fascinated with the themes of Christian faith which recur, enigmatically perhaps, but also unmistakeably, in, for example, the work of Faulkner and Beckett. In *Waiting for Godot* there are clear hints of the Good Samaritan parable as well as of Good Friday. The language of faith seems to have an attraction even though its meaning is repudiated. It may be that this is no more than the strategy of scepticism, despairing of the imitation of Christ—since the two tramps only end in the ditch themselves when they go to the aid of Lucky. Pozzo, in the same play, may even be taken to suggest a study in the frustration of 'God', for he is the 'landlord' with hints of a Divine role and appears to move, as theology might, from a powerful justice-and-strength image to a hesitant and ineffectual compassion. Is all this simply a sort of apostate's hangover? Or is there a surviving, even wistful, interest in the patterns of religion despite their complete rejection?

A positive answer is more feasible to this kind of question when we turn to Faulkner's work. Here the Christ *motif* is recurrent and compelling. The Christian tradition is freely used to illuminate or to intimate the human condition. *A Fable*, with its tale of a crucifixion, is the most obvious example. In *The Sound and the Fury*, Dilsey, the negro woman, emerged from the welter and waste of the Compson family and of Yoknapatawpha, with their imbecility, their damnation and their futility, as a redeemed and redeeming figure. Around her there gathers a complicated transposition of the events of Holy Week. Characteristically, these intimations of Christhood are not spelled out assuredly. They are left to their exemplification in simple, instinctive figures, whose invincible goodness or directness of loyalty illuminate and save the situations which no reason or abstract theology could undertake. Ike McCashlin, the childless carpenter, in *Go Down, Moses*, Nancy in *Requiem for a Nun* and Lena Grove and Byron Bunch in *Light in August* have to be construed in deeply religious terms. The Cross seems to be constantly the paradigm. Human experience is depicted, with its violence and its wrath, its frailty and pride, in a way that both requires and vindicates the historic Christian answers. There is no doubt an unanswered tension with the Stoic alternatives and there is certainly a powerful insistence that the Christian story cannot be honestly believed without responsible relation to the chaos and tragedy of men. And the charismatic souls win only partial triumphs. Waste has its way: the entail of social guilt, of southern slavery, of moral decadence, 'like beads of penance on a rosary that has no end', cannot be stayed. There is a kind of inevitability of impotence and shame which cannot be reversed.

... people, men and women, don't choose evil and accept it, but evil chooses men and women, by test and trial, proves and tests them and then accepts them for ever until the time comes when they are consumed and empty and at last fail evil because they no longer have anything that evil can want or use: then it destroys them.[1]

Yet, all the more emphatic, by this realism, are the simplicities of soul, the qualities of heart, which, by their very goodness retrieve and restore, or, otherwise, are not themselves overcome.

Two writers taken at random cannot prove a case. Nor is our point served if it is seen as a 'case to prove'. It suffices that the frontiers between belief and unbelief are seen to be much less distinct than dogmatists on either side of them suppose. There emerges a sort of believing at the heart of unbelief, a kind of trust even within the view than finds the world absurd, a will, as it were, to have it not so. If we find ourselves parting from the answers of faith, we are still alive with the questions to which they

[1] William Faulkner, *A Fable*, New York, 1955, p. 258.

have been given, if we are alive at all. The honesty with which we decline assurance remains an ingredient of its surer perception. Our very scepticisms prove an exercise in the option by which our humanity is constituted. We do not cease to be ourselves because we cannot find ourselves. Even the atheist knows himself doing duty for the God he cannot worship. He cannot make good his negations existentially. If it matters to be without meaning, then meaning, if only interrogatively, is restored. We are not brought back to any content of faith, merely by experience of its absence. But we are certainly brought again to the dimensions of faith, if only in order to sustain the life-situation which the emptiness creates. 'Bad faith,' as a total indictment in Sartre's sense, can only be a valid charge if there is a feasible integrity of human being. And that, in short, looks suspiciously like a kind of 'caliphate' of trust. It is time, then, to turn to the final section of the theme.

'BAD FAITH': MAN IN DECISION

The purpose of the foregoing was first to face, and rebut, the view that religious man is essentially compromised in integrity by the very fact of faith. Secondly, it was to take the measure of the disavowal of faith as an inherently deceptive concern for certainty and comfort and, as such, a distortion of human existence. The charge, in the one case, cannot be generalized. For, within the religions themselves with which we are concerned, belong the profoundest correctives against self-absolutizing temptations. In the second case, we have found a strange ambiguity in the concern for an honest humanity which seems to point back to possibilities it sets out to defy. Whether within or without, the charge of 'bad faith' seems to call into only clearer perspective the things it intends to call into question.

What is also clear is that there is about human existence a sort of unlimited liability, within which there are no categorical immunities. We discover a sort of Kantian awakening, not merely to the egocentric situation in respect of empirical knowledge, but to an inclusively crucial role for man in the determination of significance. We discover a sense in which everything turns upon ourselves. Yet it is ourselves that are within the verdict that we make. Existentialism in general, and the 'bad faith' indictment of religious man in particular, have the effect of inclusifying the human decision, and a making total of man's self-assessment. Man is, so to speak, at once the data and the definition. His being is a matter of his verdict as well as of his nature. He has not merely to 'organize' but to 'allow' his being. There is about him the 'given' of nature and history, of constitution and determination. Yet these are such as to admit of inward decision and to require self-ordering. Just as every man, it is said, is old enough to die, so man is in essence big enough to be. There is an inclusive autonomy which he must accept to fulfil.

We arrive, then, at a new sense and a new measure of the human privilege from which we set out at the start. If men could be suspected of 'bad faith', not in some mere commercial, social sense, but in this ultimate misconstruing, allegedly, of their existence, if they can be suspected of unworthily, self-centredly, conveniently, plausibly, falsifying the truth of themselves—as these strictures say—does not such a formulation, aside from its truth as a charge, argue a responsibility in man of ontological proportions? Does not the very onus, whether or not in detail it be sustained, assume a sort of inclusive liability in man for man?

Are we not, then, within the 'caliphate'? Even God's being is, in this sense, permissively within our decision. Certainly atheism is an option of our life and of our mind. *We* have to let God be God, for only when we thus allow our own Godwardness to be the truth of ourselves do we give God existence within our worship. He is, to that extent, God by our leave, which is, exactly, what, at its full stretch, the doctrine of the human caliphate affirmed. To say: 'Thou shalt have none other gods but Me' means that there is a sort of human prevention of the Divine. Not, of course, ontologically or in the imperative. Plainly not. Without the reality of God, the command against His exclusion could not arise. The Divine sovereignty, to use theological language, is exalted 'far above our poor power to add or detract'. In that sense, to continue with Lincoln in his different context: 'We cannot dedicate, we cannot consecrate, we cannot hallow'. The being of God is eternally and unassailably beyond our Yea! or Nay! That is the givenness of our subordination. Yet the subordination itself is such as to involve and achieve a free recognition, a decision of acceptance. It becomes itself when we allow it. In that sense, we do 'dedicate, consecrate and hallow': we do let God reign. It is in these terms that man may be said to be, not simply responsible *to* God, but responsible *for* Him. God's existence, as a human assurance, turns permissively on man's interpretation of himself. God exists if man wills it, for it is then that worship kindles. He is enthroned, as the rabbis so finely said 'upon the praises of His people'. This in no way alters or violates the reality of God: it merely explores its nature as mirrored in the dignity of man. 'At the very spring of our consciousness, we find this inseparable demand to be independent only by the right dependence, and dependent only by the right independence.' 'He will not have us accept His purpose save as our own.'[1]

The final, essential 'bad faith', therefore, is to reject either side of this stature, to refuse the proper empire by a retreat into piety, or absolutism, or arbitrary religion, or on the other hand to assert an autonomy which denies the surrender. It is to fail to hold together the kingship and the priesthood which the New Testament marries into one in its interpretation of the nature of man. There is our manifest authority over nature, made feasible by its own dependable and orderly processes, and yielding the whole plenitude of culture and art and technology. There can be no right fearing, or denying, or voiding, of this competence and creative *imperium*. To shrink from any of its elements in timidity or indifference is to deny the human meaning. Yet the priesthood must strenuously pervade them all, the hallowing by which a true gratefulness takes all things. There is no element of the empire, whether sex, or race, or nation, or territory, or reason, or power, or art, or work, or competence, or technology, which is not the truer, not to say, safer, for its being the theme and material of

[1] John Oman, *Grace and Personality*, London, 1917, quoting from the 1960 edition, pp. 65 and 68.

thanksgiving. For only so is its tributariness to us and, with it, ours to God, proclaimed and ensured.

It is just at this point that the ambiguity of current notions of 'secularization' arises. If we mean that man must possess and assert his sovereignty, that 'sacredness' is not an abstraction from life, that there are no arbitrary reservations of experience from human curiosity or human responsibility, it is valid. But if it means that man is thereby absolute, alone, autonomous and unconsecrate, it is damnable and false. Indeed, the more secularized, the more urgently to be hallowed. We can only safely risk the utmost exploitability of nature in the context of the undeviating hallow-ing of man. We properly disown the notion that sanctity belongs only to man in gardens and rustic simplicities, where some secularizers would gladly banish it. But we do so because it is a robust reality capable of informing and purging the ways and works of the machine. And that ever more urgently. For tech-nology is more and more liable to a sort of 'demon-possession' unless it is effectively related to criteria beyond its own immediate range of competence or intention. Planning on a vast scale, to avoid chaos, can readily create servitude. Techniques of mass communication may multiply information and yet promote ignorance. Means of affluence deprive initiative. Productivity threatens personality. Laws of the applied sciences operate in a context which is not neutral for their objective processes but per-verts and aggravates their consequences by a score of bedevilling perversities remote from their competence but vital to their results.

In all these ways it is clear that secularization is a menace even the secular cannot afford. Technological science is bound to take account of factors beyond technological control. The only purely technical criterion of invention, mechanization, and scientific sophistication, is feasibility. But the technically feasible is plainly no sufficient test either of the desirability or even the tolerability of the product. If we are to subdue the means we attain in any effect-ive way to the meaning of man, it can only be as man himself possesses and enforces his own dignity with the element of worship as its deepest sign and pledge. Or, in Biblical terms, creation is the external condition of the human covenant, and covenant, in turn, is the internal condition of the creation.

There have been times in the history of man when it was urgent to say, 'The sacred was made for the secular, not the secular for the sacred'. In effect, Jesus did so by caring for the palsied on the sabbath and reversing the religious outlawing of the publicans. Amos did so by condemning the forms of worship that co-existed blandly with the oppression and despoilation of the poor. Certainly the modern secularizers do so in disallowing escapist religion, sheltering behind pious comforts from the real business of the living world. It could still be, that, in places, this is the prior emphasis in the calling of man, out from false authority into the true liberty.

But manifestly, it is only half a story and there is no time, least of all the present, that is not strenuously in need of the alternate truth, 'The secular is made for the sacred, not the sacred for the secular'. 'The sabbath was made for man', truly. But this only has meaning if, properly acknowledged 'man is made for sabbaths'. Unless man is 'made' a being congenial to the sabbath benediction it has no due relation to him. Unless there is a mutual validity there can be no notion of, nor attempt at, the mutual relation. The negative part of either statement can never be absolute, but only as it were tactical and relative, depending on the current travesty. If one were to say 'Love was made for man', one can never even begin to say 'Not man for love', since here we have arrived at a perfect inter-dependence of definition.

It is almost like this with the sacred and the secular. We have neither truly, unless we have each. To lose the one is, in the end, to make man absolute and this is perdition. To lose the other is to make him abject, and this equally is to be lost from God. That 'the world was made for man and man for God' is the only true form of faith. For only then is man authentically over things and unto God. The ultimate 'bad faith' is to miss or to repudiate either the empire or the thanksgiving.

VIII

The Significant Absence
and the Real Presence

TODAY's reader of the Book of Job has good reason to be
dubious about the arguments of heaven which once seemed so
devastating against the patriarch. 'Have you entered into the
springs of the sea or walked in the recesses of the deep?' Indeed,
scoured them with submarines, churned them with depth charges
and charted them on maps. 'Have you entered into the storehouses
of the snow?' Antarctica is crossed, by sledge and tractor, by man
and machine, and Everest is climbed. 'Who has divided a water-
course for the overflowing waters . . . to satisfy the waste and
desolate land?' the architects of the Tennessee Valley Authority
and the makers of the High Dam at Aswan. 'Knowest thou the
time when the wild goats of the rock bring forth? do you observe
the calving of the hinds?' We do indeed, and from our telescopic
lenses transfer the knowledge to a million television screens. 'He
saith among the trumpets, Ha! Ha!' This kind of cavalry steed has
long been obsolete in warfare and lives only in nostalgia.[1] Other
arguments mainly from the realms of untamed nature may have
proved overwhelming to the man in the land of Uz but they
scarcely subdue the contemporary technologist.

It is, perhaps, unfair, to answer so roundly even though the
Biblical tone invites it. For there is a deep sense in which the purpose, if not the tenour, of the case abides. But we do so deliberately in order to register in these very easy terms the impact of the
enlarging competence of man upon traditional attitudes to God.
We shall pursue them later into much more taxing fields than the
obsolescence of the horse and the dam-ability of rivers. The ancient
appeal to the mystery, the majesty, the might of God and the
corresponding exposure, frailty and ignorance of man, falls on our
ears with less and less conviction. How shall we continue to say

---

[1] Quoting from Job xxxviii. 16, 22 and 25 and xxxix. 1 and 25.

with the psalmist: 'Cease from man whose breath is in his nostrils, for what is he to be accounted of?' when, whatever his transience, his science seems so effective in determining the shape of things? It is not simply that he no longer 'goes forth to his work and to his labour until the evening', but that his whole relation to environment has undergone a revolution of gathering self-sufficiency.

This cumulative autonomy of man, as it seems, argues a growing redundancy in the concept of the Divine. It is almost as if the tables are reversed: 'Cease ye from God . . . for what is He to be accounted of?' It can be argued that worship is now a dispensable dimension of our existence and the Divine an unnecessary hypothesis, that we are in fact, for all operative purposes, left to ourselves in the universe. If God exists, He is significantly absent from our affairs and the vacancy, however distressing to piety or frailty, is one that we can ourselves quite adequately fill. Experience is in fact self-supporting and is being proven the more so in the practical competence of man.

The purpose of this chapter is not only to ponder more telling examples than those of Job, but to claim from this full recognition of the human capacity to 'manage' godlessly[1] what is in fact a truer disclosure of the nature and pattern of the Divine relationship. It is to suggest that the autonomy of man, ensuing in the 'absence' of Divine intrusion, is in truth the shape of a 'presence' consistent with the stature we have all the time been arguing. The once unanswerable dominance which we encounter in the arguments of Job can be seen as reflecting the persuasions natural and compelling in his and his author's context. If they are clearly pleas in a case which can no longer be set down in those terms, this fact witnesses to our human entry into achievements then, and for long centuries, only latent. The consequent revision of the argument in Job is, therefore, topical only and not essential. The very feasibility to men of the powers which invalidate the details corroborates the essence. We may, as it were, turn the questions

---

[1] 'Manage' is not used here in any derogatory sense, but in its proper meaning of 'having in effective control'.

into the negative: 'Can you not enter into the treasures . . .' and find the theme the more, not the less, impressive.

So we are back in an intensified expression of the 'caliphate'. 'The presence of God', we may say, 'is dialectically conjoined with his absence.'[1] The growing, actual autonomy, newly ful-filling the ancient prerogatives of the human condition, means a sharpened liability, a deepened obligation. The more man 'escapes' from the Divine,[2] as the writer of Job might see it, in the ability to dispense with that dimension as party to his weakness, the more surely he finds it returning as a party to his strength. 'Going-it-alone' proves to be a sort of contradiction in itself, inasmuch as 'aloneness', whether socially or ontologically, is no context for his 'going'. We must not mistake a magnificent freedom from interference as if it were a constitution in isolation from mystery and love. Secularism, in this context, claims at once too little and too much. It magnifies the human empire but neglects the human destiny. The aloneness by which man may manipulate environ-ment and shape history is itself the setting of a larger crisis in which he is himself at stake. To know ourselves in crisis is to confess ourselves under judgement, and this is to know ourselves no longer alone.

This, however, is to anticipate. Our immediate duty is to the glad confession of the human dignity. What we abandon, theologically, when we do so, is nothing essential to an authentic faith in God, but only the oppressive, interventionist, arbitrary concept which did have currency in many minds and systems in the times of man's more modest and precarious hold upon the forces of the natural order and the menaces of the animal, or the bacterial, world. Admittedly, those intimidating and despotic notions of deity did have an immense and tyrannizing grip upon the human imagination. But it is clear they were never an authen-

---

[1] Quoted from R. Gregor Smith in 'Post-Renaissance Man' in *Conflicting Images of Man*, edited by Wm. Nicholls, New York, 1966, p. 38.

[2] 'Escapes' is, in one sense, the wrong word here, inasmuch as there is no imprisonment. We are speaking for the moment from within familiar assumptions of 'Divine tyranny' as alleged by popular writers.

tic part of the Biblical tradition. The empire of man, it is true, has taken long generations to exclude and transcend them. But the power by which it did so is the essence of the inherent dominion which we have already studied. It is the degree, not the gist, of modern technology which is unprecedented. Man is seen, Biblically and Quranically, as the being to whom such prowess is proper and natural. Its achievement has, of course, been cumulative. Nature has not told her secrets: she has simply answered his questions and waited till he put them. It would be idle to enthrone the contemporary stage of technology as if it had either marked, or occasioned, some qualitative difference in the human situation itself. For its triumphs have only been attained by steady dependence on, and indebtedness to, the centuries whose character it may too easily despise. Even where the scientific conquest has revolted in order to find liberation, it remains heir to the things it has superseded. This is true not merely in the obvious sense of the perpetual displacement of scientific theories by the new successors they generate, so that constant substitution of earlier for later knowledge is the hallmark of the scientific enterprise. It is true also of what may be superficially regarded as unscientific attitudes or habits. Magic itself, which might be thought to be in polar antithesis to the laboratory, does in fact embody the instinct to the control and subjugation of environment which is the goal of empirical investigation. Certainly the long, medieval disciplines of scholasticism, so much maligned for their pretension, their abstraction and their subtlety, did in fact constitute a long education of the human spirit in the art of rationality and in the sense of order. Both these lie as a confidence and as an instinct behind the whole scientific programme and may be said to be shapers, for all their rejection, of the modern scene.

It has needed science itself to disclose the ultimate nature of science. Its own theories have suggested its own experiments, but these have in turn jettisoned and transformed its theories. Its instrumentally crude efforts have fathered the instrumental refinements which have so transformed their consequences. There has been revolution, truly, but only by cumulative relation to the

outmoded past. Scientific history is in this way a story of precedents for the unprecedented. It is, therefore, well to abjure the
notion so intoxicating to certain modern writers that man is now
in generically different role from any previous generation. He is
simply in more exhaustive possession of his perennial dignity.

The other side of this coin is, of course, the sense of the recession
of God, or conversely, the circumstantial relations of belief in
Him. In earlier times environmental precariousness bore more
darkly and immediately upon the human spirit. Science had not
yet achieved the measure of affluent or technical cushioning by
which the burdens of disease, hunger, danger and fear have been
so widely mitigated in modern circumstances. Adversity and
tragedy were much more unpredictably and ineluctably related
to the human condition. 'I flee unto Thee to hide me' is a more
natural emotion where there is more to fear or where what might
otherwise be feared is not yet amenable to human prevention or
human control. But it is important to see this as a circumstantial,
not an essential, change in the sense of the Divine. The old fears
were never merely prudential or cringing or calculating. It was
not simply the will to survival that inspired them: they were shot
through also with awareness of mystery and awe. They were, at
their finest, an acceptance of finitude, a confession of mortality,
with which, for all his competences, modern man has still to
reckon. It is not well to dismiss a whole sensitivity to wistfulness
and creaturehood as if it were only primitive or in that sense to
decry the primitive as if it were only crude and craven.

This is not to involve ourselves here, except parenthetically,
with a related aspect of this matter of fear. It is plain that in some
measures, the actual precariousness of existence has increased under
technology. The skill which saves us from the like of the Black
Death shapes the devastation of Hiroshima. We are beyond the
fire hazards of London, 1666, with its narrow lanes, its wooden
combustibility, its innocence of pumps. But there are fires of the
1940 vintage that come fearfully from the skies, and there are
worse sorts of annihilation. The human origins of these different
perils make them at once more ominous and, in their way, more

secularizing. They are more threatening, not only by their destructive competence, but by the fact that they are derived from human passions. Their greater explicability gives them a more spiritually desolating quality. We understand them so well but, unlike the science they employ and with which we may counter, that knowledge does not make them tractable. Nor does it allow us to say so readily as of yore: 'Let us fall into the hands of God, and not into the hands of men'. But if, in this way, we are secularized even in our fears, we have come thereby into realms of human precariousness which argue all the more strongly for their salvation the effective sacredness of man.

Either way, then, the recession in the significance of God is both circumstantially impressive and essentially unreal. Rather, every new dimension of human competence is a new disclosure of human liability. As the trust extends so it also deepens. Religious naïveté may be in inverse relation to technological sophistication: but religious depth is properly in parallel progression with it. The authentic sense of the withdrawal of God is not that He may be ousted to allow our dominion, but that He may be present to our possession of it. We have been right to chasten and abandon ideas of the Divine presence that were intrusive, arbitrary and catastrophic. For these deny the order of nature and the very possibility of science. They disqualify the human condition and have no place in a right theology or a true philosophy. But the human dominion which we thereby confess in no way requires or argues the Divine exclusion. On the contrary, it is an empire which moves freely and congenially[1] in the Divine presence. It is either obtuseness, or perversity, to persist, as do some current writers for reasons of their own, in the view that the hypothesis of God is an incubus on science, an archaism of mind, a perpetuating of human immaturity, an intolerable, indefensible and inhibiting notion. That to which these charges might conceivably relate is

[1] 'Congenial' here might be open to misconception. It does not, of course, imply any neglect of the whole problem of human pretension and self-will. It is intended simply in the sense that the human is truly achieved in the context of the Divine.

quite unrecognizable to Biblical faith and bears no discernible relation, other than fantasy, to the gift and trust of human dominion. If we will only openly and imaginatively accept and conceive of our humanity, we will find ourselves well aware of the present reality of God and of how it has about it just that dimension of absence that is the context of our dignity.

There are to hand several contemporary examples of this truth of the absent/present quality in the shape of human awareness of a Godward relationship. Where the independence becomes more evident the accountability grows. The more nature becomes secularized by exploitation the more the resultant situation needs to call for urgent hallowing. The less things are circumstantial and therefore, in the old sense, Divinely attributable, the more they come volitionally within the human sphere, and the more vital, in turn, becomes the question of man and his meaning. Or, if we are to use Biblical categories, all experience involves an intensification of covenant. The more we are free and competent to do, the more crucial what we are. There is a presence of God which returns all the more surely for our independence of it.

This would seem irrefutably so in the obvious field of the technology of mass destruction. There were formerly in the grim vicissitudes of human conflict, immunities of circumstances, accidents of exemption, by which survivals might be had. But there is an ultimacy about modern capacities which turns them into a balance of annihilation. All the more shattering then the human liability for the human, when we have nothing to attenuate the decision we take about ourselves. And, if we cannot use this corporate language, then all the more are we in jeopardy. In all this, one might well wish a more fortuitous, a less efficient, situation, a fate more mercifully open, less expertly ruthless, where we might with better hope fall out of the hands of men. But technology forbids it to be otherwise and exposes us to all that either passion or folly may decide.

Or take the several far-reaching technological revisions of the circumstances traditionally obtaining to undergird the familiar patterns of ethical behaviour in the western world, based on religious belief. We now have an economic shape of things which calls into question the old 'virtues' of thrift, simplicity and diligence. There are imperatives in the very systems of production which reverse these and necessitate restless acquisitiveness and greed. The techniques of manufacture and distribution require philosophies of deliberate waste, of consumption by artificial stimulus geared to the material, at the cost of ethical, considerations. The question: what sort of people are we becoming? remains, indeed gathers urgency. But answering it adequately throws ever greater onus on the human spirit. The possibility deepens that men may not be big enough for the civilization they have engineered. Even where we seemingly obviate the need for what we used to know as goodness we make its definition all the more taxing and its achieving the more vital.

The issue, moreover, presses in a world where these affluent erosions of former mores take place in a sphere of accentuating privilege, from which whole masses of humanity are miserably excluded. We are witnessing in this decade the sort of Marxian nightmare of aggravating poverty and waxing wealth, from different reasons and with more menacing consequences than those which he foresaw. Capitalism has found a way to obviate its supposed descending spiral but not of surmounting the human prejudices of race, the passions of greed, or the accidents of geography and history. Thus it is that the less developed countries find a sharpening crisis, with the balances of trade and the advantages of technocracy running more and more in favour of the affluent against the poor, and doing so with such impetus as to make much heralded aid programmes look rather hypocritical. Within the favoured nations, economies manipulated or dominated by particular interests operate quite decisively against the minority elements. The will, if not the capacity, to find new ways of distributing the wealth of the community in the increasing obsolescence of the old assumptions of work and reward, of labour and wage, lags far behind the steadily accumulating pressures of mechanized production and cybernation. In this sphere also it would seem that technology has potentially liberated the human frame from sweat and tedium, only to threaten the human spirit with vacuity and barrenness. Unemployability is a far greater horror than unemployment, the more so if it is unrelieved by imagination in a paradox of plenty. What is technology to do about the denial of the possibilities of work and the burden of the means to leisure? Evidently, again, there is no technological answer as such, but only a fresh confrontation with the question: What are we making of our own and of our neighbour's humanity?

Nowhere is the revision of ethical norms by new factors of technology more intrusive than in the sphere of sexuality. Contraceptive devices, almost infallibly sure and readily available, mean a profound psychological and social difference in the fact of sex. Sexual experience has, thereby, the capacity to be, or to become, entirely inconsequential, its physical transactions feasibly sundered from all other spheres of its responsible relation. It may be said that prostitution, in one sense, has provided this for man through long generations. But there is a newness about this current development, a subtle shift in how the sexual may be seen in relation to the personal and the marital. Happily there are a hundred considerations to militate against general promiscuity, many of them deep in the nature of personality and in the inherent wonder of sexual experience. But several of the traditional deterrents need no longer be among them. By the same token, marriage as an institution of society undergoes a bewildering potential change with the interests of society in general in the consequences of human sexuality quite practicably diminished. Some at least of the familiar incentives to the inception of, and to loyalty within, marriage, as well as the concepts of covenant and 'estate', and of 'sacrament', for its hallowing, are radically threatened. The exchange of intimacy may be denuded of all other personal involvement than its enjoyment. But then it is no longer intimate exchange.

It may be claimed, and with some truth, that there are advantages here. A technique may serve to suspend fear, shame, anxiety, danger and deceit and so give to the sex act a welcome liberation.

Such sophistication has its benefits, not to mention the evident advantage of at least some mechanical intervention between sexual appetite and population pressure. There is, to be sure, the other side of the coin, namely the risk, if not the fact, of abstracting physical intimacies from the whole inter-play and mutuality of personal fulfilment on every level. It has always been basic to the Hebraic and Christian, and in this context the Islamic, view of marriage that the physical realm sacramentalized and 'enfleshed' what was essentially a total and unreserved will to unity in love.[1] Within that quality of commitment the new controls of the physical part of sex spell richer, and still responsible, mutuality. But outside that context, they are liable to prompt or to promote the irresponsibility that makes for the deterioration of personality, the coarsening of life and the cheating of joy.

Whatever may be finally said about the sexual liberties in contemporary western societies and the trend to the readier practice and the easier allowance of abortion—and these are vast topics beyond the present context—the point at issue is plain enough. The new situation throws an ever larger onus on the personal quality, the human self-reckoning of men and women within their own hearts and wills. As with other spheres, so here, modernity itself is a call to magnanimity, a sort of invitation to greatness. It requires what seemingly it does so little, other than the mechanical, to furnish, namely a bigness of soul, a capacity to live with the poetry of things, an instinct after the hallowing of which, in Donne's phrase, 'the body is the book'. There is nothing romantic in putting it this way. For life is constantly discovering to us that we bring too little to too much. We seize the mystery of our being with clumsy hands, avidly clutching the

---

[1] The most vital Quranic passage in this connection is Surah 30. 21. 'One of His signs is that He has created wives (or mates) for you . . . that you might live in joy with them and He planted love and tenderness between you.' While it is true that marriage in Islam is only contractual (and not an estate) it is the only proper context, aside from female slaves, for sexual relations. Though not essentially monogamous or life-long, it has a deep quality as a Divine institution and divorce is the most hateful of permitted things. See the present writer's *The Dome and the Rock*, London, 1964, Ch. 14: 'Islam and Sex'.

new devices with which ever more readily to gain, and ever more surely to dissipate, the wonder.

This is clearly the point at which to ponder the 'situation ethics' of recent advocacy, the school of thought that rejects all principles as 'heteronomy', and resists all codes or laws if they are understood as legislating inclusively for human decisions. This thinking is inspired in large measure by the compulsive sense of technology with which we have been dealing. In its view traditional standards and normative rules had their origin in static social mores and from prudential fears or demands which technology has rendered obsolete. The new capacity to do what we will has to be reciprocated by the untrammelled right to do so. Ethics, in other words, must be technologically docile, amenable to permit where science is ready to equip. A kind of empirical individualism can prevail, as for example in the sexual field, because the stake of society in the consequences is either moribund or improper. The new feasibilities somehow of themselves legitimatize the rights of individual option which absolutist ethics deny or withhold. Men, so it is claimed, should be free to decide their own conduct in the light of their private reading of the meaning of obligation and their definition of the good. Any other basis of action, it is argued, makes an unwarranted imposition on the human spirit and degrades the human dignity. Man cannot rightly be motivated by authority outside himself. 'Thou shalt' and 'thou shalt not' are an insufferable incubus and frustrate a true maturity.

It may be conceded that theologically based ethics have sometimes generated an unhappy conformism and conduced to servile or unexamined attitudes. But these advocates of moral individuation take the case beyond all limits of sanity, for the chief reason that it does violence to human community. It is intelligent to see in principles and codes a sort of formulation of precedent in human experience. Let us properly disown a purely slavish acceptance of their dicta. For they are rightly to be taken only on conviction and not on mere assertion—and in respect of 'theological ethics' this dimension of 'loving the law' is always present. The Torah, for example, is not essentially command but invitation; it is an exchange of covenant in which Divine authority anticipates human collaboration. Its framework is liberty through law and law in liberty. Given the right reasons within the structure of commandment, we may properly see the obligation as a formulation of the precedents that make for human fulfilment and the authoritative structure may freely serve their attainment.

Clearly if the injunction to love is paramount—as the situation ethics school agrees—then love's behaviour in the given human situations does not begin to be apparent only to my contemporary genius. It has plainly been sought and followed by long sequences of men of like passions with myself. No true good is ever in that sense unprecedented and there is no 'unprecedentedness' about the times of a sort to disturb that fact. The precedents, therefore, of compassion, of sacrifice, of mercy, of justice, of simplicity, of humility, and all the rest, avail for my time and place, by virtue of the commonness of our whole humanity. We must distinguish between the fresh and exacting achievement of these precedents in the new situations we handle and the fictitious novelty of our own humanness. To cut ourselves off from the gathered experience of the whole is a quite irresponsible pretension. Nor does its vaunted 'aloneness' really enable the virtues it admires. For these, in most circumstances, need the discipline, the objectivity, the tradition, the imitation of Christ, the communion of saints, which are elided in the refusal of all 'heteronomy'—all motivation, that is, that addresses me from without or with the tones of obligation.

It is, of course, dangerous, and in the end defeatist, to argue that people are not big enough for this kind of total freedom, this ethics of potential, or actual, novelty. That way lies the subtle tyranny, the plausible slavery, of Dostoevsky's Grand Inquisitor, arraigning Christ for calling men to too large a liberty. Insofar as 'situation ethics', with their will to autonomy, intend that repudiation, they are right. But there is no necessary logic moving from that rejection to a disqualification of all proper authority, least of all in Christ. In its proper postures, the setting of command, of obligation, addressing our human dignity, not decrying it either by dictation, as the absolutists, or by flattery, as the situationists, serves to the achieving of both law and liberty. To be 'a man under authority' is no violation of our being, when the authority is right. Situations are not novel, and the antithesis between autonomy and heteronomy, pushed this far, violates the wholeness of man.

These are issues deserving a fuller story. What suffices in context is the point that the more we engross ourselves in the question of ourselves the more utterly we find a dependence within our very independence, a constraint within our true liberty, a presence that abides in the very assumption of its absence.

We sharpen the case further if we glance, however briefly, at that other theme of our technological fertility, the multiplication of drugs. In responsible medical and social discipline, they take their place, beneficently and mercifully, in the panoply of human powers. They constitute a newly compelling instance of our caliphate. But in their personal utilization they open up a quite awesome dimension of human decision about humanness. They make possible experimentation with states of existence in such sort as to put new measures to the old question: 'To be or not to be'. The evasion of the 'real' world, or ambiguity as to what or where it is; distortion, abeyance, manipulation, or simply experimentation, of personality; suspension, or steady atrophy, of relational existence by abstraction into some private realm of fantasy or euphoria; the resultant wastage or wreckage of human nature —all these are the actualities which open up before us, with the further prospect of their proliferation, given technological inventiveness and their accentuation, given human wistfulnesses and commercial perversities, within the ever sharpening tensions and pressures of contemporary living and its insistent incentives to escapism. It is not simply the likely social burden of the incidence of psychedelic drugs in naïve or peevish users, or from profiteers in greed, that looks so threatening: it is the larger liabilities of our current civilization in trust with its own crisis.

It may be said that there were anodynes before—work, or drink, or exotic islands, or the like. Or there were wretchednesses that simply bred and festered without sophisticated licence to express or shape themselves and that, therefore, the human condition is not more essentially distressful. To set against the gloom are the sober potentials of the new competences. But these are brave and hardly convincing answers to the case. Whatever the issues are to mean, it can scarcely be questioned that they intensify the task of keeping faith with what we are, assuming that we know it. Things are the more unequivocally in our hands by the very capacity to decline them. A presence haunts us in the very duty to face ourselves.

And suppose we take to the planets into non-human realms of newness. Our humanity precedes us there in the very intention. Whatever awaits there deserves to be protected from the bacteria which, without due care, we might introduce. Our ethical obligations already belong and obtain where we have not yet arrived. There is no escaping ourselves and the irony will only be the more insistent if we achieve this extra-terrestrial adventure out of a world that cannot look upon its own cities without shame. The moon is no salvation from our own garbage or astronauts a sufficient symbol of human destiny.

These slight, even random, musings—not presuming to be more—would be inexcusable outside the single purpose of the present argument, which is to take the technological accentuation of the human predicament, see it as proceeding in what may be appropriately taken as the absence of God and yet in that very quality bearing clear signs of His presence. We do not mean any easy assumption that the human situation *has* to be Divinely related if we are to do justice to its crisis. Much of the foregoing fits potentially into alert forms of humanism. What we do mean is that there is a quality in our whole experience, as technology both equips and imperils it, by which its responsibility, precisely in being to itself, is also beyond itself. We are called actively to be ourselves, yet somehow within a charter of their meaning which is already given. In venturing the one we are always within the reality of the other. When we most proceed upon our self-sufficiency it is most deeply disproved. The ultimates we are free to ignore stay for us to recognize them. We can discern the Divine reference of ourselves as an option we can neglect but not as a meaning we can deny.

There is illumination for us, beyond certain of its now obsolete details, in the underlying philosophy of Marx and his view of history as human 'externalization' tending ever towards the threat of human alienation by, and within, it. Many of his presuppositions are close to the central thesis of this whole book, as to man in dominion. The Hebraic heritage of the architect of Communist theory is no accident or coincidence. Nature is the realm of man's proper exploitation, of which civilization is the result. The world here is viewed as that by which man makes himself fully man. It is the domain of his fabrication of tools, the employ and extension of his senses and the territory of his conquests. History is this human self-realization, by the processes of production that arise from man's quality as labourer, artificer, tool-maker and economic imperialist. All other imperialisms, of course, derive by extension from this fundamental theory of the labour origin of all wealth and value. Nature, then, in a way that, in a different sense, Keats, for example, would have agreed, is human nature: it is the external, material form of that which in man is the will to empire. This, as we have seen in Biblical and Quranic terms, is creation for covenant, covenant with creation. It is the effective duality of things and men, the substance and the sum of history. Technology, in terms familiar to Marx, and now far beyond them, is the ever intensifying thoroughness, precision and mastery of exploitation and production. We need not stay over what is historically outmoded in Marx, to seize upon his crucial belief, namely that man, in his productive possession of nature, brings forth that which threatens humanness, and does so, not merely by the perversion of the processes to traditional contentions of race or territory or malice, but more deeply in that he objectifies inhumanly. He transacts his ends with the natural order in such wise as to oppose humanity both in himself and in other men. This is the recurring theme of 'alienation' in the thought of Marx, with roots both in philosophic determinism and economic theory.

Man is alienated, then, even in fulfilment. The nineteenth-century sign of this was the world of industrial Manchester, where for the most part, with other corroboration, the emotional impetus of Marx was generated. As a deep cry of pain, his socialism saw humanity confiscated as it were by human works. Capitalism marked the domination of egoistic demands and by its nature dehumanized not only those it made its victims but those it made the victors. Whereas in Hegel's system there was a sense of the subject/object relation as *in itself* an alienation of spirit to be overcome by history, Marx taught that the human aliena-tion lay in the compulsiveness of production, the despotism of money and the aberration of 'private property'. Man's life has been subordinated to his existence.

The less you are, the more you have; the less you express your own life, the greater is your externalised life—the greater is the store of your alienated being. Everything the political economist takes from you in life and in humanity, he replaces for you in money and in wealth. Money . . . is the true endowment. Yet being all this, it is inclined to do nothing but create itself, buy itself; for everything else is after all its servant. And when I have the master I have the servant and do not need his servant. All passions and all activity must therefore be submerged in greed.[1]

This economic 'loss of the self' through the patterns and the existing laws of production, Marx proposed to change in that con-text. While at times he argued the self-alienating self in much further and deeper reaches of existence, it was the social, not the ultimate, aspects of it which he was set to reverse by economic rather than intra-personal salvation.[2] So doing he intensified the predicament by the very forcefulness of the economic salvation he proposed. Yet he had rightly sensed that human existence had sorer contradictions against human life than Communism allowed.

'When I have the master, I do not need his servant' was how

---

[1] Quoted by Robert Tucker, *Philosophy and Myth in Karl Marx*, Cambridge, 1961, pp. 138–9, from Marx and Engels, *Historisch-Kritische Gesamtausgabe, erste Abteilung*, Vol. 3, p. 130.

[2] See the illuminating comment in Tucker, *op. cit.*, p. 149.

Marx put the dehumanizing nature of capitalism. The whole of our case here, and the reason for citing him, might be abridged into the saying: 'When I am the master, I need not stay the servant'. This is the crux of the alienation of man in its total sense, and by the same token the clue to its retrieval. Technology only sharpens the temptation and makes the right confession the more imperative. Every enlargement of the human *imperium* is a new impulse to submission, every attainment of power over things a fresh occasion of the true worship under God. It is not so of necessity, only that it may be so by consecration: the ultimate of our responsibility is the measure of our liberty. The values that inform the human situation await our recognition yet imperatively define our nature. This is the meaning of the absent and the present God. Only in His worship do we truly humanize our humanity, and meet not only the menace Marx identified of economic alienation, but of the deeper personal and social alienation we experience in our very self-sufficiency.

We are fortified in this conclusion by the reflection that other attempted solutions develop their own nemesis and frustration. There is historical revolution itself and the temptation by which it absolutizes its own urge. Nowhere has this been more eloquently argued than by Albert Camus in *The Rebel* and other works. Man by his very refusal of any kind of slavery goes far beyond that single act and challenges a whole universe, in that, with his defiance, awareness and aspiration, potentially total, are released. Such a mood and such an achievement are within our very secularity in what Camus calls 'an unsacrosanct moment of history'.[1] So far so good. There is a clear reaching out towards totality both of humanity in solidarity and of meaning in its fullness, when men 'rebel in order to exist'. Yet the very militancy breeds its own perversion. In defying with Promethean courage what it takes to be the evil thing, it is betrayed into a selfishness which requires in turn a new Promethean repudiation, unless that is, it learns moderation and subdues itself. Then it will be served

---

[1] *L'Homme Revolté*, trans. by A. Bower, 1956 edition, New York, p. 21.

by the eternal verities. Or, in Camus' distinction, it will be, not revolution, but rebellion, not an anger in ultimate defiance of life, but a passion on behalf of life.

Only when we rebel do we sufficiently disown what otherwise we would imply to be absolutes of history. But if we deify the very insurrection which denies them we enthrone our own pretension. 'The only original rule of life today: to learn to live and to die, and, in order to be a man, to refuse to be a god', sets out in his characteristic trenchancy the essential relativity of all man's institutions, whether of affirmation or rejection.[1] The belief of the faiths of synagogue, mosque and church would be that man is only 'not a god' when God is worshipped. Camus' rebel 'rejects divinity in order to share in the struggles and destinies of all men'. He goes on:

The earth remains our first and our last love. Our brothers are breathing under the same sky as we; justice is a living thing. Now is born that strange joy which helps one live and die, and which we shall never again postpone to a later time. On the sorrowing earth it is the unresting thorn, the bitter brew, the harsh wind off the sea, the old and new dawn.[2]

If only we correct the view that the sense of the Divine means the postponement of the living joy and surmount the suspicion that to acknowledge God is to acquiesce in fear, or timidity, or history as other than it is, then this lyricism may speak also for the confessors of His name. But, either way, we and all our works must know that 'a limit under the sun must curb us all', if ever we are truly to possess ourselves.

The Jew, the Muslim and the Christian, however, reckoning with Camus in this sense, are not honest if they do not allow that religion too, including their own, has been implicated in these false absolutisms—religion perhaps most of all. Some aspects of

[1] *Ibid.*, p. 306. His fear that faith is somehow 'romantic postponement' is natural but by no means necessary. See below. In another passage, he says that to 'put the responsibility for justice in God's hands' is to consecrate injustice (p. 287).
[2] *Ibid.*, p. 306.

this we have already faced in the previous Chapter. It was part of Marx's philosophic ancestry that he saw religion in the familiar terms of anti-human tyranny, subverting a right humanity by buttressing the dehumanizing structure of capitalism by sanctions of quiescence or worse. In this diagnosis, linked with Feuerbach, the alienation of the human happened by dint of the demands of the Divine. Necessarily, on this view, God could only survive by the deprivation of man. Worship was essentially impoverishment. Man had to be diminished, by this account of faith, in order that God might be exalted. The Divine honour could subsist only by the human enslavement. If God were to be all, men must be nothing. The more emphatically this mutual relation of Divine sovereignty to earthly squalor was understood the more effectively would its institutional expression facilitate the economic corollaries with which it had conspired.

It is useful to contemplate this travesty for the double reason that it runs in dark contrast to the whole conviction of our argument and that it exposes, none the less, a tragic perversity of belief. Both illuminate the significance of a Divine absence within a real presence.

On the first score, it suffices to recall from Chapter II, that the myth of Satan's rebellion turns on his disavowal of Divine wisdom through a disdain for the human creature. Sovereignty in God is in that way staked in the dignity of man. The related notion of the caliph proceeds upon this same concept. There is an entrustment of what is God's in what is man's. Marx's charge, however originated from actual religion, has no semblance of truth by Semitic criteria. At this point, of course, the Christian understanding of the Incarnation deepens the rejection even further. For it lives by the conviction that the human is capable of being the dwelling of the Divine and when we see how that human is we cease to find it unworthy of God. This is the Christian significance of the Christ and the ground, as we saw, of all human 'sonship'. Judaism and Islam, plainly, could not go so far and their reservations are reverent. But things in which they are by their very character involved are closer to the Christian view than they have often realized. For the mystery of the Incarnation is no more, and no less, than the climax of all religious mystery, whether of creation, or revelation, or prophethood, or law. For in each and all of these, that of which in belief we say 'of God' is 'with men'. Part of the wonder of the Incarnation is that it so insistently and inclusively occupies the central point of all religious paradox.

But whether confident here, or reverently sceptical, it is all the same towards the Marxist notion of antipathy. Whether we move with the metaphors of Lord or shepherd, King or Father, or *Raḥmān* or *Raḥīm* as Quranic invocation uses them, all are akin in the conviction that the Divine relation is a human enrichment and the human response a Divine joy. That is not Divine in the name of which there is alienation of the human.

Yet the passionate honesty of Marx is enough to warn us that the distortion happens. Indeed, its possibility is no strange tidings to Jew, or Muslim or Christian. The Lordship in the Bible and the Qur'ān is always alive to the alienation man suffers by the alienation worship commits. For this is the essence of idolatry. Worship itself undergoes a usurpation, and becomes itself, in its forms, or shrines or means, the perverted end. Then an institutionalized and captive deity arises, the 'God' against God, to counter whom we must always seek the God beyond 'God' and know our very concern for Him a possible evasion of His claims. How this might be discerned in the narrative of Abraham we have tried to understand. It is an alertness which lies deep in the whole tradition we have been exploring. It is in this sense that much of the contemporary suspicion of religion, whether vehement as in Communism, or wistful as in Camus, or aloof as in Somerset Maugham, is an ally of the theist.[1] It surely sustains our whole case if it be seen that to worship falsely is to perjure ourselves. Only under the true Lordship have men the right being.

It is perhaps well to add that the rational in man is not of itself a sufficient detector or subduer of these false absolutisms. Reason

---

[1] 'Aloof' of Maugham in the sense that story-telling is the beginning and the end, the picture not the saving. When he has described he is (his own phrase) 'rid of it'.

itself, in Luther's graphic phrase, may be 'a whore', and has the habit too readily of being prostituted by wrong motives. Here too the very technological expertness of our time hides a sinister ambiguity. Vested interests easily usurp the true functions of reason and turn it into a perverse persuader, a manipulator of words, a servant of demons. The command to 'love the Lord with all your mind' stands as a perpetual validation of the right role of reason in a sound theology. To hold only a functional, pragmatic or instrumentalist view of the rational in man is to invite its worst distortion. If it can do no more than 'serve' other elements in man, then its servility is already near. It only finds its dignity in its converse with God, and for this it is well endowed. But that splendour of the rational, whereby truth is loved, must not obscure the Biblical conviction that it only happens so in the wider setting of the love of the Lord 'with heart, soul and strength'. Hence the emphasis, throughout the Hebraic, Christian and Muslim ethos, on history and action, revelation and event, devotion and commitment, as the ultimate context of the Divine-human encounter. 'God, not of the philosophers', as Pascal has it, but 'of Abraham'. It is not simply by the rational awareness of our state that we shall rightly reckon with it. Knowledge may be power in the achievements of science: but it is not salvation, unless it be the knowledge of God, and this must turn on more than mind.

So we come to the end of the road. We have confined ourselves to man, his liberty and his tragedy, possessing all things yet somehow ever at a loss about himself. The theme of him in the Semitic faiths seems to have come round full circle, in the contemporary realization of a dominion unparalleled in his history, yet also intensified in its vexation. There is no retreat into past simplicities. There is no escape from the acceptance of the empire. But the courage of a present affirmation of man can only be sustained in the recognition of his tributary meaning, in the humility that senses and obeys the reality of God, as at once the source and the goal of the human meaning. We have on hand, in this time and generation, a crucial battle for the renewal of the sacred, for the new authentication of the eternal relation of our being. 'A town without intimations: in other words completely modern', was how Camus described Oran.[1] He went on to locate that lost dimension in 'men and women consuming each other rapidly in what is called "the act of love"' or, alternatively, settling down in 'mild conjugality'. In his passionate way, he sensed that somehow humanity had lost itself on both counts, the cheap or the humdrum, the casual or the crippled. People, he thought, in Eliot's phrase, for whom nothing had ever happened.

Magnify the onus of his lament, as it deserves, to its ultimate length, as honesty demands. For the 'intimations', once we admit them, will carry us forward into themes of praise and benediction where it would be false, even to the first of them, to refuse to follow them to the end. And then we shall back in God, the inclusive 'intimation'. He is absent that He may be freely sought, present wherever He is found. Our secret in Him is not compulsive, only free: we find, only when we seek, and love truly only in knowing we are loved. We need the courage to extensify within the whole the implications of our personal being and see the universe as meant for just that courage. Many will see this an 'anthropocentricity' and dismiss it with either a shrug or a fear to be cheated. Those who refuse either attitude and take the faith-option do so loyally, not conceding that they have engaged in wishfulness, but contending—a hypothesis just as authentic as any reservation—that this very shape of personality is itself responsive to just such a kinship, as inseparable from its own reality. We do not then derive God from man, or faith from wistfulness, in any originating sense, but only because men themselves are already derived, in their very seeking, from Him they find.

But the battle for the Divine dimension is strenuous in the extreme. It may be easier when men, in their contemporary exuberance of conquest, have got beyond the notion that they have somehow done so by denying Him. Thinking that we have to live as if God did not exist, as if there was only ourselves, is no

[1] Albert Camus, *The Plague*, translated by S. Gilbert, London, 1948, p. 72.

new discovery, properly seen, nor is it any ground for an inclusive loneliness of man. It is simply the rather intoxicating, modern form of the authority by which man has always been responsibly constituted to his own environment, no matter how primitive, how impressionable (in Job's sense) his *imperium* may have been. The point, simply, is that the intensification of applied competence is mistaken for some new constitution of affairs, from which God has evacuated, and not solely a novel, and exciting, form of unchanged human potentiality. It may be hoped that we shall yet surmount the naïveté that supposes God to be more categorically absent than the human dominion has always experienced Him relatively to be. In that event, we shall not need to indulge any further the illusion that in fulfilling our empire we have abrogated our worship, or that we have only become what we are by an emancipation from God. On the contrary, man has known in fuller degree what he has always been and the experience leaves him not less, but more, in fealty.

'Mightn't it be better for God if we refuse to believe in Him?' Camus once asked.[1] Certainly many beliefs and believers have done Him ill service. He is well disembarrassed of the evasive timidities, the deep hypocrisies, the chronic self-pities, the introverted pieties, the irresponsibility, out of which men call upon His Name. But the more effectively we call men to die to this kind of divinity, and let it die to them, the more insistently we return towards the worship which kneels and wonders and hallows and adores, precisely because it cares widely, loves sacrificially, dies hardly and lives courageously. In that recognition, the living God has many seekers who seem not to know His sign, or might want in His very name to take it with suspicion. But these have their place in His unwearied patience, for their pains are part of His own jealousy for truth. So dependable yet so deferential to our spirits is that patience, that we may reverse the question and enquire: 'Mightn't it be truer for themselves if they began to seek Him?' For that seeking is no 'raising of our eyes toward heaven where He sits in silence', but the taking in hand of the human

[1] *Ibid.*, p. 144.

enterprise as willed by His mercy, guided by His word, and left at issue in our hearts. 'Let God be God' is at once a command that meets us and an option that we hold. And in both senses it is the secret of our own reality.

The Epistle of St James has always seemed something of an unusual document in the New Testament, the odd letter out perhaps in a collection from more dominant hands. Yet it contains a passage well fitted to conclude our thoughts.

Be doers of the word and not hearers only, deceiving your own selves. For if any man is just a hearer of the word, and not a doer, he is like a man looking in a mirror and seeing the face of his birth who from the glance goes off and forgets the fashion of his humanity. But any one who looks hard into the perfect law, the law of his liberty, stays with it and does not forget what he hears but translates it into action, he is the man for whom, in action, the blessing will come true.[1]

It is, at first sight, a puzzling argument, especially that phrase about 'his natural face'. It can hardly mean what he personally looks like. For who is there who ever really forgets this? Is there a white in Johannesburg who does not remember that he is so, or a negro in Chicago who is allowed to forget? Do people really become oblivious of their own features? The sense, and the Greek, are more subtle: 'the face of his birth', not 'his own face', but rather 'the proper truth of his being'. What he forgets is not his race, nation, colour, but the humanity into which he was born, the dimension of his human nature. There is an evident link with i. 18: 'He begat us with the word of truth that we might be . . .' He gave us being by His initiative with a view to a certain destiny. This calling the man glimpses in a fleeting way. He contemplates his freedoms and his laws, his potential and his reckoning. But the passing awareness is not taken up steadily into life. He relinquishes the secret he dimly discerns and so doing, 'goes his way', cheating,

---

[1] James, i. 22–5. Some have ingeniously suggested that there is an accent on 'what *man* . . .' with the inference that no woman would ever forget what the mirror told. But this is too inventive. There is much in classical ethics about mirrors of self-examination: when the truth is ugly one should be humble, when it is handsome, grateful!

depriving himself, by a sad 'misinference' (i. 22) about his life. But by translating the true vision into life and deed, the attentive hearer fulfils his humanity with benediction and delight. 'Be you doers' refers, not to some mere 'carrying out of orders', but rather to a kind of poetry of existence, that has learned the true rhythm of the line and metre and found itself in the discovery. 'Be you poets of the word' is the literal translation, and for once the literal is the profoundest of suggestions. It is the things that are bound which are most surely free, the musician with his score, the flier with his craft, the singer in his song. These too are the liberations of science, found only in submission. These, all, are 'blessed in their poetry'.

So it is, in their several ways, with Torah, with rule and with Gospel. Men have to consent to their identity. Their liberty is in the Divine law. The competence of man in technology grows progressively more spacious and awesome. It is the more urgently to be rooted in 'the law of the Lord'. Our contemporary society looks more critically than any other, into a larger mirror than them all. And we take our way, privilege in hand, either to lose or to find. For that is the law and the liberty.

INDEX

1. Subjects and Authors

2. Biblical References

3. Quranic References